IN
SEARCH
OF TRUTH

CHUCK GROSS

IN SEARCH OF TRUTH

A Layman's Guide to Catholic Spirituality

Hickory Hill Press
Nashville, Tennessee

Nihil Obstat: Most Reverend David R. Choby, S.T.B., J.C.L.
Bishop, Diocese of Nashville
January 24, 2007

Imprimatur: Most Reverend David R. Choby, S.T.B., J.C.L.
Bishop, Diocese of Nashville
January 24, 2007

The *Nihil Obstat* and *Imprimatur* are a declaration that a book or pamphlet is considered to be free from doctrinal or moral error. It is not necessarily implied that those who have granted the *Nihil Obstat* and *Imprimatur* agree with the contents, opinions, or statements expressed.

Permissions:
hickoryhillpress@yahoo.com

In Search of Truth is available at special quantity discounts for bulk purchase for church or school promotions, premiums, fundraising, and educational needs. For details, write Hickory Hill Press Special Markets at hickoryhillpress@yahoo.com.

ISBN-13: 978-0-9839158-2-9 (paperback)

Cover photo of the Istanbul Hagia Sophia (Ayasofya) Deesis mosaic courtesy of Dick Osserman.

I dedicate this book to all the great saints and spiritual authors whose writings have helped me in my search for understanding and truth. And to my mother, who introduced me to my faith and showed me by example how to live it in my daily life.

"Silence is the language of God."
Anonymous

Author's Note:

I have written *In Search of Truth* with the hope that the information gathered within will be of spiritual value to the reader. My intent, besides giving a layman's explanation of how to awaken one's faith, is to provide a spiritual source where the reader not only reads through the chapters as one reads a normal book, but takes the time to meditate on and seek the true understanding and beauty of the Scripture passages and the writings of the saints and Church Fathers quoted in this book. The reading and meditation of these passages can become a prayer in itself. From these meditations, readers should be able to take their new gained knowledge and use this understanding to better judge their day-to-day actions with the intent of living a more rewarding spiritual life.

Scripture selections are taken from the *Douay-Rheims Bible* translated from the *Latin Vulgate*. The Old Testament was first published in 1609 by the English College at Douay. The New Testament was first published in 1582 by the English College at Rheims. It was revised and annotated in 1749 by Bishop Richard Challoner.

I have tried to write *In Search of Truth* in a simple, direct, and easily understood manner. Please forgive any shortcomings and understand that I am a servant of our Lord and love Him and His Church.

CONTENTS

PART TWO

Prayers and Meditations

INTRODUCTION

Man throughout the ages has wondered, "Why am I here?" Great thinkers like Aristotle and St. Thomas Aquinas spent their lives searching and studying to find the answer. Even though it is a simple four-word question, I have, throughout my life, asked the same question and have spent a good part of my life searching for the answer.

I was raised in the Catholic faith and remained active in my faith throughout my teens and adulthood. I believed I was a good Catholic attending Mass on Sundays and trying to live a decent life. But as with most people living in our secular society, my main focus in life was on establishing my career, finding a wife, and having children. I decided, upon graduation from school, to become a pilot. I put my determination and dedication into becoming one and have had a successful career flying for a major airline. I got married at twenty-five and have been blessed with a beautiful wife and two daughters, who are now grown.

I have spent most of my life practicing martial arts and have been teaching Southern Praying Mantis Kung Fu for several years. In my late forties, I started doing a meditation called *Zhan Zhuang*, which in Chinese means "standing like a tree." (It is pronounced "Jam Jong.") This med-

1

itation consists of standing perfectly still in different postures for various lengths of time, followed by a sitting meditation for an equal length of time. As I progressed in this Eastern form of meditation, I found myself being drawn closer to God.

One night during my sitting meditation, I had a vision of a beautiful, young woman. Her head was covered with a scarf, and all I could see was her face. Her expression was what touched me. It is hard to convey in words how it affected me other than to say I felt a feeling of pure non-carnal love. She appeared in my mind for a few seconds and then quickly disappeared, but her expression did not fade. I can still close my eyes today and see her beautiful expression. Not having the proper knowledge to understand this vision, I could feel my meditation becoming disturbed, but I continued to meditate.

A few weeks later, I had a vision of Jesus nailed to the cross. Instead of the cross being upright, the cross was laying on the ground with Jesus nailed to it. I began to worry. What was happening to me? Was it just my imagination? Who could answer my questions? I continued my daily meditation, but during my days off from flying, I started doing research about visions. My research brought me to a book titled *The Collected Works of Saint John of the Cross.* St. John had been a Catholic priest back in the sixteenth century. He was a contemplative who had written several papers on achieving union with God while on earth. His advice concerning visions was to disregard them first, because they can become a distraction from your meditation, and second, because you do not know their source. I read all of St. John's works in search of a better understanding of what I had experienced. His readings led me to the writings of St. Teresa of Avila, who was also a sixteenth century contemplative.

I continued my meditation, and as I read more about visions, mine stopped but something else started happening, which instead of being pleasant, was very painful. When I would start my sitting meditation, within minutes, I would feel a sharp pain in the right side of my back as if I were being poked with a burning hot needle. This pain would become so severe during my meditation that at times I could not continue to meditate.

At the same time as this was happening, I attended Mass at a local church across town from my regular parish. The church's priest was visiting Rome, and a young visiting priest was filling in for him and saying Mass. By his appearance, I would have estimated that he was in his early-to mid-thirties. Unknown to me at the time, this young priest's sermon, combined with what had been happening during my meditation, would lead me on a search that would change my life forever.

When it came time for the homily, Father went to the pulpit and introduced himself. He explained to the congregation that he was going to speak about things they would not want to hear and would most likely find offensive. This statement immediately caught my attention, as I'm sure it did others. As he began his homily, it quickly became apparent why some parishioners would take offense at what he was saying. But at the same time, it became very clear to me that what he was preaching was truth. The trouble is most of us do not want to hear truth. We like to think we do, but in reality most of us do not.

The priest spoke on topics that I had not heard addressed from the pulpit in years, if ever. He covered topics like sex, which I have never heard a priest talk about to this degree in a sermon. He spoke about sin, hell, and even about masturbation. He explained how years ago the lines for Confession were longer and the lines for Communion were shorter, but now very few people go to Confession, yet everyone goes to Communion. He then asked, "What does this mean?" He went on to explain that this indicated that we believe that sin no longer matters. The more he spoke, the more I became stirred up inside.

As he continued to talk, he spoke of death, a subject that I thought I knew well. Death had played a major part in my early life. When I was eight years old, I had watched my father die of cancer. The cancer was savage and took only three months to end his life. My mom was left a widow with five boys to raise, ages three to twelve. When I was eighteen, my grandmother who lived only a block from us, passed away. Her son, my uncle, died within three months of her death. He had been a good brother to my mother and had given her much moral support while she was raising us boys. At the age of nineteen, I went to Vietnam as a U.S. Army helicopter pilot. During my tour, I saw the ravages of war and death many times and lost some good friends.

As I listened to this young priest preach about different sins, the effect that these sins have on our soul, and the punishment that these sins deserve, I knew and understood that he was speaking truth. When he stated very simply that the cause of death was sin, I realized that I didn't really understand death at all!

I asked myself how I could be forty-nine years old and not understand death. I understood that sin injures our relationship with God and if we die with grievous sin on our soul, we are banished to hell, but what I was hearing was so much more than that. My understanding and knowledge of death was more on a physical death of the body rather than a spiritual death of the soul. As I meditated on his statement "Sin is death," I came to the realization that this was profoundly true. During my own life, I have seen what people accept as truth change. Relativism was creeping into Christianity, conveying to Christians that there are no moral absolutes. Truth was becoming harder to find.

After Mass, I did a lot of soul searching on what this young priest said. I realized that I had fallen into this lackadaisical feeling about sin. I had not been to Confession in years, convinced that I could just ask God for forgiveness and everything would be okay. I realized that with this approach, I seldom thought about sin. When we don't think about our sins, we tend not to ask forgiveness. A few days later, I went to Confession with this young priest. During my confession, it became clear to me that a new door had been opened, and I was on my first steps of a journey that would take me in search of what truth is.

Chapter 1

SEARCHING FOR GOD

A sk the average person the question "How do you find God?" The answer most likely will be one of the following: read the Bible, attend a prayer service, or go to your local church. In my search for truth, I have discovered that even though all of these choices are useful for spiritual growth, none of them is in itself correct.

If you want to find and know God, you should go directly to Him. You begin by searching your own heart and soul. If you take the time seriously to explore the love and feelings within your heart, you will awaken your soul, for the two are connected. Your soul is your spiritual connection between God and your human body.

God is never farther away than your intellect. A simple thought or a brief prayer will help awaken a sense of God's presence within you. God exists in every human being, no matter how evil that person may be. In the book of Genesis we read, "*And God created man to his own image: to the image of God he created him: male and female he created them*" (Gen 1:27). We understand that since God does not have a physical body, this divine image refers to a spiritual image known as our soul. St. Paul tells us, "*Know you not, that you are the temple of God, and that the Spirit of God dwelleth in you?*"(1 Cor 3:16). St. Paul understood this indwelling presence of God to be within all mankind.

As you search within for your spiritual connection to God, be sure to ask in prayer for God to send down the Holy Spirit to help guide you in your search. "*But the Paraclete, the Holy Ghost, whom the Father will send in my name, He will teach you all things, and bring all things to your mind, whatsoever I shall have said to you. Peace I leave with you, my peace I give unto you: not as the world giveth, do I give unto you. Let not your heart be troubled, nor let it be afraid.*" (Jn 14:26-27). Ask the Holy Spirit to enlighten your soul and allow you to feel the inner presence of God. If you're sincere and truly seek union with the Father, the Lord will answer your prayer. Psalms 34:16 reads, "*The LORD has eyes for the just and ears for their cry.*" This lets us know that God listens to our prayers. Jesus told his disciples, "*Amen, amen I say to you: if you ask the Father anything in my name, he will give it you*" (Jn 16:23).

To find God is to journey toward Him. St. John of the Cross says, "Unless they go in search for God, they will not find him, no matter how much they cry for him." [1] In your journey, you will use daily prayer, meditation, Scriptures, and the Church that He founded, to help guide you to communion with Him. The journey is like a trek through the mountains. One day you experience the beauty of the mountaintops in all their splendor, and the next, you may feel the loneliness of the sunless valleys. But as in any journey, what is important is that you keep moving forward. It is a hard journey; the Lord Himself says: *"How narrow is the gate, and strait is the way that leadeth to life: and few there are that find it"* (Mt 7:14).

To know God is to love God, and to love God is to live the Gospels. Two Doctors of the Church, St. John of the Cross and St. Teresa of Avila, both teach that we cannot love and develop a spiritual union with God if we do not live the Gospels. Jesus tells us, *"Not every one that saith to me, Lord, Lord, shall enter into the kingdom of heaven: but he that doth the will of my Father who is in heaven, he shall enter into the kingdom of heaven"* (Mt 7:21). The Letter of James says, *"What shall it profit, my brethren, if a man say he hath faith, but hath not works? Shall faith be able to save him? And if a brother or sister be naked, and want daily food: And one of you say to them: Go in peace, be ye warmed*

---

[1] St. John of the Cross, "The Spiritual Canticle," *The Collected Works of Saint John of the Cross*, (Washington, D.C.: ICS Publications, 1991), 490.

and filled; yet give them not those things that are necessary for the body, what shall it profit? So faith also, if it have not works, is dead in itself" (Jas 2:14-17). By living the Gospels, we are on the correct path to union with the Father. *"Jesus answered, and said to him: If any one love me, he will keep my word, and my Father will love him, and we will come to him, and will make our abode with him"* (Jn 14:23).

Our secular society places many distractions in our path that hinder our journey toward God. When we have to go against the norm of society, it becomes very hard, especially when raising children, to follow God's teachings and live the Gospels. When we live in a society that frowns upon moral truths and holds up personal choice over ethical behavior, it becomes an even greater challenge. The media conveys the message that immoral behavior is okay. "It is a woman's right to have an abortion. Homosexuality is normal, and gays should be allowed to marry just like everyone else." The majority of movies and television shows portray couples having sex on their first date or living together, while persons upholding traditional morality are portrayed as intolerant and unhappy. It is hard not to be tainted by so much immorality. Think of how this must affect our children, especially when they are in their teenage years. We must resist letting these enticements to moral decay pull us away from God's teachings. Do not condone this type of behavior, nor accept it as being okay. Do not give up hope. Scripture tells us that the journey will be hard but the reward will be great. *"But love ye your enemies: do good, and lend, hoping for nothing thereby: and your reward shall be great, and you shall be the sons of the Highest"* (Lk 6:35).

To bring God into our lives, we need to start thinking about Jesus and how He lived His life as an example for us to follow. In spare moments, I will recite this little prayer: "God, I love you. Jesus, I love you. Blessed Mary, ever virgin, please pray for me." If you start saying a short prayer like this one several times a day, you will be surprised at what a change it will bring to your relationship to the Father. I have found through my own experience that if something upsetting happens to me shortly after I have recited this prayer, I end up reacting differently to the situation than I would have if I had not been thinking of God.

Developing a personal, loving relationship with the Father requires proper guidance. This is very important if we are to advance in spiritual union with Him. Jesus tells Peter, James, John, and Andrew, *"Take heed that no man seduce you: For many will come in my name saying, I am Christ. And they will seduce many"* (Mt 24:4-5).

Where do we find proper guidance? First, from God Himself. God will help guide us on our spiritual journey with the power of the Holy Spirit. All we must do is ask Him in prayer. *"Ask, and it shall be given you: seek, and you shall find: knock, and it shall be opened to you. For every one that asketh, receiveth: and he that seeketh, findeth: and to him that knocketh, it shall be opened"* (Mt 7:7-8). Start out every morning by asking our Father to send down the

Holy Spirit upon you to guide you in your daily journey.

Secondly, we can find guidance through the one true Church that Jesus started on earth. "And I say to thee: That thou art Peter (Kepha), and upon this rock (Kepha) I will build my church. And the gates of hell shall not prevail against it. And I will give to thee the keys of the kingdom of heaven. And whatsoever thou shalt bind upon earth, it shall be bound also in heaven: and whatsoever thou shalt loose upon earth, it shall be loosed also in heaven" (Mt 16:18-19).[2] God gave us His bridegroom, the Church, to help interpret His written Word and to guide us in our spiritual journey. We know from Scripture that the Church is the pillar and foundation of truth. "But if I tarry long. That thou mayest know how thou oughtest to behave thyself in the house of God, which is the church of the living God, the pillar and ground (foundation) of the truth" (1 Tm 3:15).

Thirdly, through Scripture reading, prayer, and meditation, we learn how God wants us to live our lives. When studying the Bible, it is important to first learn what the different books of the Bible are and how the Scriptures are

---

[2] My intent is to not write a book on apologetics, but some Christian denominations will try to counter this Scripture by explaining that in Greek the word *Petros* means a small pebble or stone and *Petra* a large massive stone. Either they choose to ignore or are ignorant of the fact that Aramaic was the spoken language of Jesus, and Matthew was originally written in the Hebrew tongue, most likely in Aramaic in which the word *Kepha* means the same as *Petra*. The Rock.

grouped together. St. Thomas Aquinas in his *The Inaugural Sermons* gives a great sermon on Sacred Scripture. To interpret Scripture correctly, you must first understand why each book was written, to whom, for what purpose, and then finally in what style. Without this knowledge, it is easy to be led astray.

Finally, great guidance can be found from the early Fathers of the Church and the Saints. By studying their writings and lifestyles, we can learn invaluable lessons in developing our relationship with the Father. It is always best to learn from one who has already achieved what we are trying to accomplish.

We have been given several resources from our Father to learn and understand how He wants us to live our lives. It is up to us to do the searching and then follow through with action.

To find God is to find love. When the Pharisee lawyer asks Jesus, "Master, which is the greatest commandment in the law? Jesus said to him: Thou shalt love the Lord thy God with thy whole heart and with thy whole soul and with thy whole mind. This is the greatest and the first commandment. And the second is like to this: Thou shalt love thy neighbor as thyself. On these two commandments dependeth the whole law and the prophets" (Mt 22:36-40). Jesus is telling us that the most important commandment is to love God above all things. This should become our first priority in life. It must come before our love for our spouses, families, money, and our jobs. This is what Scripture refers to when it tells us not to put other gods before the Father. How many people do we know that put their love for money above their love for God? To them, their money becomes their god. Too many, their love for drink, drugs, food, or sex becomes their god; still others worship sports, entertainment, popularity, recognition, or worldly success.

The Lord's second commandment is "to love your neighbor as yourself." This does not mean that we have to like our neighbors and agree with their actions. To be able to do so would be against human nature and would be impossible to achieve. This commandment simply means that we must love our neighbors and forgive them for their shortcomings, and if necessary, be willing to give our lives for them. This may sound hard to do, but we actually see it happen in combat when we have two soldiers who dislike each other, yet one ends up giving his life for the other. This is true love. Jesus gave us such a great example of this love when He died on the cross in order that all mankind might have eternal life. For most of us, reaching this degree of love will be an ongoing and even life-long struggle, but we can be sure our efforts in this regard are very pleasing to God.

Chapter 2

PRAYER

An absolutely essential part of achieving and sustaining a Christian life is prayer. Without prayer, there can be no spiritual life. Jesus, the God-Man, spent hours in prayer with His Father. In Luke 6:12 we are told, *"And it came to pass in those days, that he went out into a mountain to pray, and he passed the whole night in the prayer of God."* His disciples learned from Jesus' example how important it is to develop a strong prayer life.

Regular prayer is the key to establishing spiritual union with God. This is very important to understand. How can we develop a deep relationship with our Father if we do not share our thoughts and time with Him? It is the same with a relationship to a friend, spouse, or child. If we stop communicating with each other, we will find ourselves growing apart, and the relationship suffers. So it is with our relationships with God.

Through reading Scripture, we learn that God wants us to pray.[1] Mathew 7:7 tells us, *"Ask, and it shall be given you; seek, and you shall find; knock, and it shall be opened to you. For every one that asketh, receiveth: and he that seeketh, findeth: and to him that knocketh, it shall be opened."* We also learn that He will not force us to pray. Saint Augustine verifies this when he says, *"God wishes to give, but only gives to him who asks."*[2]

God has given us free will, which allows us to choose for ourselves whether we want to seek a loving relationship with Him. It is up to us individually to decide. It is so easy to make excuses, to tell ourselves that we are too busy working, going to school, or raising our families to find time to spend with the Lord. But this is not true. If we take a moment to consider how much time we spend watching television, reading the paper, playing sports, exercising, or talking on the telephone during our average week, we will realize that we do indeed have time. If we truly want to begin living a more spiritual life,

---

[1] Mt 6:9, Lk 11:9, Jn 16:26, Col 4:2, Rm 12:12,1 Pet 4:7.
[2] St. Alphonsus Ligouri, "The Necessity of Prayer," *The Great Means of Salvation and Perfection*, 1, 1.

we can start by making our prayer life our first priority.

How should we pray? Jesus tells us that it is best to go off to a quiet area. The fewer distractions we have, the easier it becomes to pray. Being alone also prevents us from falling into the trap of praying to impress others, which Jesus warns us about in the book of Matthew. *"And when ye pray, you shall not be as the hypocrites that love to stand and pray in the synagogues and corners of the streets, that they may be seen by men: Amen I say to you, they have received their reward. But thou when thou shalt pray, enter into thy chamber, and having shut the door, pray to thy Father in secret: and thy Father who seeth in secret will repay thee"* (Mt 6:5-6).

Most prayer should be directed to God the Father. It can be directed to the Father through Jesus. The Catholic Church teaches that it is always good to start a prayer by the invocation of Jesus' holy name. An example: "Lord Jesus Christ, Son of God, have mercy on me, a sinner."

Many people forget the Holy Spirit when praying and pray only to Jesus. But both Scripture and the Church teach us not to forget the Holy Spirit (also traditionally known as the Holy Ghost). Paul tells us in his First Letter to the Corinthians, *"And no man can say The Lord Jesus, but by the Holy Ghost"* (1 Cor 12:3). The Church invites us to invoke the Holy Spirit as the interior teacher of Christian prayer. We should ask daily for our Father to send us the Holy Spirit to guide and instruct us on our spiritual journey. In Luke 11:13 we read, *"If you then, being evil, know how to give good gifts to your children, how much more will your Father from heaven give the good Spirit to them that ask him?"* This tells us that God will send the Holy Spirit to help us. All we must do is ask. The Holy Spirit will give us strength and guidance on our journey.[3]

There are many types of prayers and ways to pray. What may work for one person may not work for another. We must find our own spiritual path to communicating with the Father. St. Teresa of Avila writes that once we start down our path, the Lord will lead us in ways that are pleasing to Him.

Spiritual exchange is very important in prayer. To many people, prayer is a one-sided conversation. They do all the talking, and God does all the listening. If you were able to have conversations with some of the greatest and smartest men of history, like Abraham Lincoln and Albert Einstein, would you do all the talking? Or would you listen and learn? It should be the same with our Almighty Father. How much could He teach us if we only learn to listen?

For years I would hear people say, "Jesus told me this" or "God told me that", yet even though I prayed daily and went to church regularly, He never spoke to me. I would tend to discount them as over-zealous fanatics, yet it made me ask myself, "Why didn't God talk to me, or was God talking, and I wasn't listening?" Learning to listen in prayer is one of the major steps in advancing our prayer lives.

---

[3] See Chapter 15 for a list of the gifts of the Holy Spirit.

How is this accomplished? By rethinking and understanding exactly what prayer is, and what different types of prayer are, we can learn how better to communicate with God. The Church teaches us that there are different types of basic prayers. We will begin with the Prayer of Petition. Simply stated, "petition" means to seek or request. It is always best to start a prayer of petition by asking for forgiveness. This asking of forgiveness calls to mind our sins and offenses against our Lord that have become part of our daily lives. By mentioning our offenses, we are able to work all the harder at recognizing and overcoming our daily temptations. The Church teaches that asking for forgiveness is a prerequuisite for pure prayer. This asking of forgiveness from God shows our humility and brings us back into communion with the Father and the Son, Jesus Christ, and with one another, so that "we receive from him whatever we ask." [4] After our asking for forgiveness, we are now ready to make our petition to God.

A second type of prayer is called the Prayer of Intercession. With the prayer of intercession, we pray on someone else's behalf. As Christians, we must be concerned with our neighbors' welfare as much as our own. Jesus taught us that the second greatest commandment is "to love your neighbor as yourself." What better way can we show love for our neighbors than by praying for them? I personally believe that praying on someone else's behalf benefits us more spiritually than praying on our own behalf. A very valua-

---

[4] CCC, (Catechism of the Catholic Church) Part 4, Sec. 1: 2631.

ble goal to attain as a Christian is to learn to pray for our enemies. Jesus teaches us this by His own example when He says, *"Father, forgive them, for they know not what they do"* (Lk 23:34). Praying for our enemies is indeed very hard to do. It tends to go against our fallen human nature, but if we can learn to do so sincerely, we are on the correct path of learning to love as Jesus loved.

Another form of prayer is called the Prayer of Thanksgiving. By thanking God for what he has given us, we acknowledge our understanding that everything we have comes from God. Paul tells us in 1 Thessalonians 5:18, *"In all things give thanks: for this is the will of God in Christ Jesus concerning you all."* When things are going well in our lives, it is easy to forget to give thanks. In our weakened nature, we tend to go to God in our sorrows and forget Him in our times of happiness. The next time you receive that new job, promotion, new house, or car that you have been saving for, take the time to acknowledge and thank God for your good fortune. Make this a habit, and it will bring you closer to our Lord.

> **"Jesus does not demand great deeds. All He wants is self-surrender and gratitude." – St Therese of Lisieux (AD 1873-1897)**

I believe one of the least prayed prayers, when one is praying alone, is the Prayer of Praise. The *Catechism of the Catholic Church* tells us,

Praise is a form of prayer, which recognizes most immediately that God is God. It lauds God for his own sake and gives him glory, quite beyond what he does, but simply because HE IS. It shares in the blessed happiness of the pure of heart who love God in faith before seeing him in glory. By praise, the Spirit is joined to our spirits to bear witness that we are children of God, testifying to the only Son in whom we are adopted and by whom we glorify the Father. Praise embraces the other forms of prayer and carries them toward him who is its source and goal: the "one God, the Father, from whom are all things and for whom we exist.[5]

This Prayer of Praise can be heard in the hymns and spiritual songs that are sung at Mass and Christian worship. Another form of praise is called adoration. In your own prayer life, you can praise God by reading the Psalms. A good way to do this is to memorize a few favorite psalms and recite them during the day, giving praise to our Lord.

Prayer can be classified as communal or private, as vocal or interior. Most people are taught as children to recite vocal prayers. They tend to pray prayers of petition for themselves and their family and friends, forgetting except in

---

[5] Ibid., 2639.

special circumstances prayers of thanksgiving and praise.

Prayer's number one purpose is to awaken love for our Lord and to achieve our salvation. Through prayer we receive God's grace and favor, which helps us to combat our daily temptations. Prayer should be a two-way exchange between God and ourselves. To ensure that we achieve a two-way communication when praying, it is best to have a Bible available. Go to a quiet place where you will not be distracted by noise or movement. Begin by making a sign of the cross (In the name of the Father, and of the Son, and of the Holy Spirit, Amen), and then start your prayer by invoking the name of Jesus. Example: "Lord Jesus Christ, Son of God, have mercy on my soul." Then follow by asking for forgiveness for your sins. Example: "Lord, please forgive me for my weaknesses and offenses against you." Now, you can pray the "Lord's Prayer" or prayers of petition, intercession, thanksgiving, or praise. (See Part Two Section B for examples.)

When you have completed your initial prayers, it is time for God to communicate to you. Take your Bible in hand. This will allow God to communicate to you through Scripture. I suggest when starting out that you read from the New Testament. Read a verse, and then close the Bible and meditate on what you have just read. After you have meditated on the verse, remain sitting or kneeling, and listen in silence. You talk to God in prayer, and He talks back to you in Scripture and silence. Pray some more, and then do another reading, followed by more meditative thought and listening. Practice saying your prayers in this manner, and you will get out of the habit of one-sided praying in which you do all the talking and none of the listening. Always be sure to include prayers of praise and thanksgiving.

In beginning prayer, it is very important that you do not allow your thoughts to wander. As you mediate on the readings, try to stay focused on the topic of the reading and explore what lessons Scripture could be teaching you. Remember, if your mind wanders off, do not be discouraged, but return to your prayer. The Church teaches that in meditation, you engage in thought, imagination, and emotion with a desire to discover what our Lord wants you to know and do. Meditation takes a lot of hard work. Practice to stay focused. Again, do not be discouraged if you find your thoughts darting off in different directions; as long as you return to the subject of your prayer (as many times as necessary), the Lord will be very patient with you.

As far as meditative methods are concerned, there are no right or wrong ways to meditate. There are hundreds of books teaching different methods of meditation, but remember, a method is only an aid. The important thing is to try to meditate daily, allowing the Holy Spirit to help you advance. If you truly pray to God in earnest from your heart and soul, God cannot help but send the Holy Spirit to help and guide you along your path. This we can be sure of, for God helps and rewards those who seek Him.

We have already learned in Matthew that it is very important to pray with humility and sincerity.[6] In His Sermon on the Mount, Jesus teaches us how to pray: *"Our Father, who art in heaven. Hallowed be Thy Name. Thy Kingdom come. Thy Will be done, on earth as it is in Heaven. Give us this day our daily bread. And forgive us our trespasses, as we forgive those who trespass against us. And lead us not into temptation, but deliver us from evil. Amen"* (Mt 6:9-11). Known as the "Lord's Prayer" or "Our Father," this is one of the best and most well known prayers.

> **"Much more is accomplished by a single word of the Our Father said, now and then, from our heart, than by the whole prayer repeated many times in haste and without attention." -- St. Teresa of Avila (AD 1515-1582)**

A good way to pray the "Our Father" is to pray the prayer according to sentence structure. Every time you come to a punctuation point, stop and meditate on what you have just prayed. For example, pray "Our Father." Then stop and meditate on why we say "Our Father." Ask yourself about God and why we call Him Father. How do you perceive Him? Do you see Him as all-loving, almighty, and all-merciful? Do you see Him as your father, teaching and guiding you through your life? Mentally picture

---

[6] Mt 6:5-6.

24

yourself in God's presence. How would you act? Ask yourself, what kind of relationship you have with Him versus what kind of relationship you would like to have with Him.

When you are finished praying "Our Father," then go on with "who art in heaven." Meditate about Heaven. Do you really believe in Heaven? Picture what Heaven is like. Do you think you will go there? What has God taught us that we must do to get there? What can you do in your present life to help ensure your path? What have you done in your past that you are ashamed of and should ask forgiveness for? How can you change your current life to better please our Lord? Continue praying each phrase of the "Our Father." By praying the Lord's Prayer in this manner, one can spend from a few minutes to an hour to recite the prayer. Much can be learned of God's will by meditating on the Lord's Prayer. (Needless to say, it's much better to pray the "Our Father," or any other prayer, just once in a slow and respectful manner, than to race through it many times in a half-hearted or distracted way.)

My two favorite writers on obtaining spiritual union with God are St. John of the Cross and St. Teresa of Avila. They were both sixteenth-century mystics, and because of their great writings on the subject of prayer and contemplation, they were honored many years after their deaths with the title Doctor of the Church. I would recommend their writings for anyone serious about improving his or her prayer life. Of all the spiritual books I have read, *The Collective Works of Saint John of the Cross* is my favorite. I find St.

Teresa's writings easier to read and comprehend and think they would be better for beginners.

St. Teresa teaches us that meditating on the Life of Jesus and especially His Passion is one of the best methods of meditation. *"This method should be the beginning, the middle and the end of prayer for all of us: it is a most excellent and safe road until the Lord leads us to other methods, which are supernatural."*[7] By meditating on Jesus' life and His suffering, we discover the great love that God, who is the source of everything good, has for us.

Prayer, like any other worthy venture, is hard work. There is no easy path to spiritual union with God on earth. One must strive to overcome distractions and negative thoughts as one tries to reach out to God through prayer and meditation. St. Teresa warns us *"that one must never be depressed or afflicted because of aridities or unrest or distraction of the mind."*[8] The harder you work at your prayer life, the more of a threat you become to the devil, and the harder he will work to distract you. (Scripture teaches us very clearly that the devil exists, and that as the enemy of our souls, he works for our spiritual destruction.)

I cannot tell you how many times I've been in prayer when suddenly the worst thought or doubt about my faith would cross my mind. These thoughts appear to come suddenly from nowhere and are very disruptive to my spiritual

---

[7] Teresa of Avila, *The Life of Teresa of Jesus* (New York: Doubleday, 1991), 144.
[8] Ibid., 133.

peace. The physical pain that I have felt in my meditation has been so painful that I have had to stop because I could not focus on anything but the pain. Through the writings of St. John and St. Teresa, I have come to realize that it is Satan casting these pains and putting doubts into my mind. During your journey, do not give into these distractions or feelings of unrest, and continue forward. Pray for the Holy Spirit to be your guide, to give you the strength to fight these distractions.

St. Teresa instructs us that one of the best ways to concentrate our minds in prayer is to learn to find where God has revealed Himself to those who love. 1 John 4:16 tells us, *"We have come to know and to believe in the love God has for us. God is love, and whoever remains in love remains in God and God in him."* St. Teresa says that focusing on God's indwelling presence in ourselves is the best way to stop our minds from wandering in prayer. [9]

Guigo the Carthusian writes concerning prayer, *"Seek in reading and you will find in meditating; knock in mental prayer and it will be opened to you by contemplation."* [10] What is contemplation? Father Thomas Dubay writes in *Fire Within* that *"Christic contemplation is nothing less than a deep love communion with the triune God. By depth here we mean a knowing loving that we cannot produce but only receive. It is not merely a mentally expressed 'I love You.' It is a*

---

[9] Teresa of Avila, *The Way of Perfection* (New York: Doubleday, 1991), 183-185.
[10] Scala Paradisi: PL 40, 998.

wordless awareness and love that we of our-selves cannot initiate or prolong."[11]

Contemplation is a non-verbal prayer. It is a prayer of quiet, of inner stillness and calm. Mother Teresa of Calcutta, a holy woman of our age, says, "If we really want to pray, we must first learn to listen, for in the silence of the heart God speaks."

---

[11] Thomas Dubay, S. M., *Fire Within* (San Francisco: Ignatius, 1989), 57.

Chapter 3

WHY THE SAVIOR WAS NEEDED

In the search for truth, it is common to question, "Why did God send down His Son to die for us?" Genesis 2:15-17 tells us, *"And the Lord God took man, and put him into the paradise for pleasure, to dress it, and keep it. And he commanded him, saying: Of every tree of paradise thou shalt eat: But of the tree of knowledge of good and evil, thou shalt not eat, for in what day soever thou shalt eat of it, thou shalt die the death."* When Adam and Eve broke God's one commandment and ate fruit from the Tree of Knowledge of good and bad, they cast mankind into corruption and death. The book of Wisdom says, *"For God created man incorruptible, and to the image of his own likeness he made him. But, by the envy of the devil, death came into the world: And they follow him that are of his side"* (Wis 2:23-25).

One of God's punishments for eating the fruit from the Tree of Knowledge was mortal death to the human race. This punishment separated man from his God and held all men captive. But God, who is all good and all loving, gave man a chance to overcome the punishment of death and regain everlasting life. How did He accomplish this? By the Word becoming flesh.[1] God sent Jesus (His Son), the God-Man, to earth to live amongst man and teach us God's (the Father) intentions and desires. Jesus, the Word made flesh, suffered and died for all mankind so that our sins could be forgiven. But more importantly, He rose again so that we could defeat the bonds of death and be able to reunite with the Word and live forever in the kingdom of God.

Since Jesus' resurrection, we now have the choice to live forever in union with God or to choose death through the wages of sin.[2] It is our choice to go to Heaven or to go to Hell. *"His disciples came to him, saying: Expound to us the parable of the cockle (weed) of the field. Who made answer and said to them: He that soweth the good seed is the Son of man. And the field is the world. And the good seed are the children of the kingdom. And the cockle are the children of the wicked one. And the enemy that sowed them,*

---

[1] Jn 1:1, 14.
[2] Rom 6:23.

is the devil. But the harvest is the end of the world. And the reapers are the angels. Even as cockle therefore is gathered up, and burnt with fire: so shall it be at the end of the world. The Son of man shall send his angels, and they shall gather out of his kingdom all scandals, and them that work iniquity. And shall cast them into the furnace of fire: there shall be weeping and gnashing of teeth" (Mt 13:36-42).

To help explain why man needed a savior, one of the great Doctors of the Church, St. Athanasius, Bishop of Alexandria AD 296-373, writes,

It is we who were the cause of His taking human form, and for our salvation that in His great love He was both born and manifested in a human body....But men, having turned from the contemplation of God to evil of their own devising, had come inevitably under the law of Death. Instead of remaining in the state in which God had created them, they were in the process of becoming corrupted entirely, and death had them completely under its dominion. For the transgression of the commandment was making them turn back again according to nature; and as they had at the beginning come into being out of non-existence, so were they now on the way to returning, through corruption, to non-existence again. The presence and love of the Word had called them into being; inevitably, therefore when they lost the knowledge of God, they lost existence

> *with it; for it is God alone Who exists, evil is non-bearing, the negation and antithesis of good.*[3]

Why was Christ the perfect offering to defeat our mortal death? In John 15:13 Jesus tells us, *"Greater love than this no man hath, that a man lay down his life for his friends."* When the Word made flesh surrendered to death His human body as an offering and sacrifice, it was the perfect offering because no mere human being could make such an offering. Christ sacrificed His perfect body free of any stain of sin. Disobedience to God gave man death. Obedience to the Father from His Son gave mankind the chance to regain eternal life with the Father. St. Paul says, *"For by a man came death, and by a man the resurrection of the dead. And as in Adam all die, so also in Christ all shall be made alive"* (1 Cor 15:21-22).

Since Christ's death and resurrection, we now have a choice between life and death. How do we do this? By doing what Jesus taught us. *"But he said to him: What is written in the law? How readest thou? He answering, said: Thou shalt love the Lord thy God with thy whole heart, and with thy whole soul, and with all thy strength, and with all thy mind: and thy neighbour as thyself. And he said to him: Thou hast answered right. This do, and thou shalt live"* (Lk 10:26-28). To choose eternal life is to choose to live our lives in conformity with Jesus' teach-

---

[3] St. Athanasius, *On The Incarnation*, (Crestwood, NY: St.Vladimir's Seminary Press, 2000), 29.

ings. Simply stated, always strive to choose good over bad. It is important to remember that when we disobey what God has taught us to do through Scripture and tradition, we are doing the same as Adam and Eve. We are choosing disobedience (sin) over God, and thus we are choosing death. Sin is what prevents us from entering eternal life with God. *"And if thy hand scandalize thee, cut it off: it is better for thee to enter into life, maimed, than having two hands to go into hell, into unquenchable fire: Where there worm dieth not, and the fire is not extinguished. And if thy foot scandalize thee, cut it off. It is better for thee to enter lame into life everlasting than having two feet to be cast into the hell of unquenchable fire: Where their worm dieth not, and the fire is not extinguished. And if thy eye scandalize thee, pluck it out: it is better for thee with one eye to enter into the kingdom of God than having two eyes to be cast into the hell of fire: Where the worm dieth not, and the fire is not extinguished"* (Mk 9:42-47).

Let's summarize why God sent His only Son, our Savior, to die for us and then to be resurrected on the third day. Before man was created, mankind was nonexistent. We as individuals are the same: until we are conceived, we are nonexistent. No doubt at the moment of conception, the Word infuses us with a soul. God made man to praise and honor Him. When man broke God's commandment and chose disobedience over obedience, that spiritual link to God was severed. Without a spiritual link to achieve union with God, death entered the world. To repair this broken link to God, a perfect sacrifice was needed. God being all just and loving sent His Son. When the Word became Flesh and then offered itself as the perfect sacrifice in death and then rose again, the link was restored. Through Jesus' death and resurrection, man was freed from the bonds of death and became free to choose everlasting life by joining his soul in union with the Father.

Chapter 4

THE ROAD TO SALVATION

Two of the most misunderstood terms when speaking with Christians of different denominations are "born again" and "saved." I have found through experience that these terms can have different meanings to different denominations.

Let's start with the term "born again." When I was a youth minister, I asked my high school youth group how many of them were born again. Three youths raised their hands. Of the three, two were Protestant and one was Catholic. The rest looked at me as if the term "born again" did not fit within their Catholic faith. I was not surprised by their answer because "born again" is more a Fundamentalist term and not a term commonly used in Catholicism.

Let's look at the term "born again" and what it means. John 3:3-6 tells us, *"Jesus answered, and said to him: Amen, amen I say to thee, unless a man be born again, he cannot see the kingdom of God. Nicodemus saith to him: How can a man be born when he is old? Can he enter a second time into his mother's womb, and be born again? Jesus answered: Amen, amen I say to thee, unless a man be born again of water and the Holy Ghost, he cannot enter into the kingdom of God. That which is born of the flesh, is flesh; and that which is born of the Spirit, is spirit."* The Church and its Fathers have always taught that this passage is referring to baptism of water through which all Christians are born again in the saving grace of Jesus Christ. We read again in Titus 3:5, "he saved us, by the laver [bath] of regeneration, and renovation [renewal] of the Holy Ghost." St. Paul tells us in Romans 6:3-4, *"Know you not that all we, who are baptized in Christ Jesus, are baptized in his death? For we are buried together with him by baptism into death; that as Christ is risen from the dead by the glory of the Father, so we also may walk in newness of life."*

In this baptism of water and spirit, we are born again into the saving grace of God with all past sins being forgiven. Colossians 2:12-13 states, *"Buried with him in baptism: in whom also you are risen again by the faith of the operation of God who hath raised him up from the dead. And you, when you were dead in your sins and the uncircumcision of your flesh, he hath quickened together with him, forgiving you all offences."* We are told that this baptism of water and spirit gives us a new life or a clean slate, so to speak, for entry into a spiritual union with God. St. Paul says, *"Know you not that all we who are baptized in Christ Jesus are baptized in his death? For we are buried together with him by baptism into death: that, as Christ is risen from the dead by the glory of the Father, so we also may walk in newness of life"* (Rom 6:3-4).

What is this newness of life that St. Paul speaks of? In the sacrament of Baptism, the recipient receives a remission of his sins. For an adult, it would be a remission of original and any actual sins that he had committed. For an infant, it is a remission of original sin. Since the child has not reached the age of reason, the child would not have any actual sins. Besides the forgiveness of sin, St. Peter tells us, the recipient, that we receive the Holy Spirit. *"Peter said to them: Do penance, and be baptized every one of you in the name of Jesus Christ, for the remission of your sins: and you shall receive the gift of the Holy Ghost"* (Acts 2:38). In Acts 11:16 we read, *"John indeed baptized with water but you will be baptized with the Holy Spirit."* In our Baptism, it is forgiveness of sin and reception of the Holy Spirit that gives us this newness of life.

Let us look at the word "saved" and exactly what it means to a Christian. Ephesians 2:8-9 states, *"For by grace you are saved through faith, and that not of yourselves, for it is the gift of God; Not of works, that no man may glory."* This tells us that we are saved by grace. But we must not stop there but continue to read verse 10, which tells us that we must live in our good works. *"For we are his workmanship, created in Christ Jesus in good works, which God hath prepared that we should walk in them."*

We are told in Romans 3:24 that we are justified freely by God's grace through redemption in Christ Jesus. When Paul and Barnabas come to Jerusalem to meet with the Church and Peter about the Gentile mission, Peter in Acts 15:11 reaffirms the Church's beliefs: *"But by the grace of the Lord Jesus Christ, we believe to be saved."* So as Catholics, we believe that we are saved by grace from God through the redemption in Christ Jesus.

Is faith alone in Jesus Christ enough to get us to Heaven? Can we accept Jesus as our Savior and then continue to live a sinful life, ignoring the Gospels and still expect to get to Heaven? Not according to Sacred Scripture or what the Catholic Church teaches. Martin Luther (whose challenge to Church teaching and practice began the Protestant "Reformation" in 1517) was the first to teach the concept of "faith alone" as the requirement to get to Heaven. This teaching was introduced during the Reformation some fifteen hundred years after the resurrection of Christ.

Does a Christian who really believes in the Blessed Trinity (the truth that in the unity of the Godhead there are Three Persons, the Father, the Son, and the Holy Spirit) think God would allow His Holy Church, which the Son of God started and the Holy Spirit guides, to be misguided for almost sixteen hundred years before sending Martin Luther or John Calvin (another early Protestant leader) to correct it? I'm not speaking of the sinful way of man, which we all fall under, even priests, bishops, and Popes. I'm speaking of the guidance of the Holy Spirit in the teachings of Christ and His apostles and in the development of the dogma of the early Church. In Matthew 16:18-19 we are told, *"And I say to thee: That thou art Peter, and upon this rock I will build my church. And the gates of hell shall not prevail against it. And I will give to thee the keys of the kingdom of heaven. And whatsoever thou shalt bind upon earth, it shall be bound also in heaven: and whatsoever thou shalt loose upon earth, it shall be loosed also in heaven."*

It is one thing to protest against the sinful ways of man, but it is heresy when we deliberately change what has been accepted as divine revelation in both Sacred Scripture and Sacred Apostolic Tradition to accommodate our own feelings. To change divine revelation is to change God's Word.

What does Scripture say about faith alone and the loss of salvation? In Matthew 25:31-46, Jesus tells us that we will be judged by our works:

And when the Son of man shall come in his majesty, and all the angels with him, then shall he sit upon the seat of his majesty. And all nations shall be gathered together before him: and he shall separate them one from another, as the shepherd separateth the sheep from the goats: And he shall set the sheep on his right hand, but the goats on his left. Then shall the king say to them that shall be on his right hand: Come, ye blessed of my Father, possess you the kingdom prepared for you from the foundation of the world. For I was hungry, and you gave me to eat: I was thirsty, and you gave me to drink: I was a stranger, and you took me in: Naked, and you covered me; sick, and you visited me: I was in prison, and you came to me. Then shall the just answer him, saying: Lord, when did we see thee hungry and fed thee: thirst, and gave thee drink? And when did we see thee a stranger and took thee in? Or naked and covered thee? Or when did we see thee sick or in prison and came to thee? And the king answering shall say to them: Amen I say to you, as long as you did it to one of these my least brethren, you did it to me. Then he shall say to them also that shall be on his left hand: Depart from me, you cursed, into everlasting fire, which was prepared for the devil and his angels. For I was hungry and you gave me not to eat: I was thirsty and you gave me not to drink. I was a stranger, and you took me not in: naked and you covered me not: sick and in prison and you did not visit me. Then they also shall answer him, saying: Lord, when did we see thee hungry or thirsty or a stranger or naked or sick or in prison and did not minister to thee? Then he shall answer them, saying: Amen I say to you, as long as you did it not to one of these least, neither did you do it to me. And these shall go into everlasting punishment: but the just, into life everlasting.

In James 2:17 we are told, *"So faith also, if it have not works, is dead in itself."* This tells us that faith alone without works is dead. James continues to explain,

But some man will say: Thou hast faith, and I have works. Shew me thy faith without works; and I will shew thee, by works, my faith. Thou believest that there is one God. Thou dost well: the devils also believe and tremble. But wilt thou know, O vain man, that faith without works is dead? Was not Abraham our father justified by works, offering up Isaac his son upon the altar? **Seest thou that faith did cooperate with his works and by works faith was made perfect?** *And the scripture was fulfilled, saying: Abraham believed God, and it was reputed to him to justice, and he was called the friend of God.* **Do you see that by works a man is justified, and not by faith only?** *And in like manner also Rahab the harlot, was not she justified by works, receiving the messengers and sending them out another way? For even as the body without the spirit is dead: so also faith without works is dead* (Jas 2:18-26).

41

James tells us quite clearly that what Martin Luther was trying to teach is not scripturally based. Many people are surprised when they read that Martin Luther actually inserted "alone" to his translation of St. Paul's doctrine of justification by faith to justify his belief.[1]

Let's look at what some of the early Christians wrote about works being a part of our salvation. St. Clement of Rome, the first Father of the Church, writes in his First Epistle to the Corinthians in AD 98, *"Seeing then that we are the special portion of a Holy God, let us do all things that pertain unto holiness, forsaking evil speakings, abominable and impure embraces, drunkennesses and tumults and hateful lusts, abominable adultery, hateful pride. For God, He saith, resisteth the proud, but giveth grace to the lowly. Let us therefore cleave unto those to whom grace is given from God. Let us clothe ourselves in concord, being lowlyminded and temperate, holding ourselves aloof from all back biting and evil speaking, being justified by works and not by words."*[2]

Origen in the year AD 226 reaffirms what James teaches us when he writes in his *Commentary on John*, *"Whoever dies in his sins, even if he profess to believe in Christ, does not truly believe in Him; and even if that which exists without works be called faith, such faith is dead in itself, as we read in the Epistle bearing the*

---

[1] Patrick Madrid, *Surprised by Truth* (San Diego, CA: Basilica Press, 1994), 129.

[2] English translation by J. B. Lightfoot.

name of James." [3] We hear it again from St. Hippolytus of Rome when he states, *"And in like manner, the Gentiles by faith in Christ prepare for themselves eternal life through good works."*[4]

Scripture tells us that after accepting Jesus as our Savior, our salvation can still be lost. Matthew 24:13 tells us, *"But he that shall persevere to the end, he shall be saved."* It does not say that all are saved but that we must persist in a state of grace till the end to be saved. It is the condition that our soul is in at our physical death that matters. In St. Paul's Letter to the Romans 11:22, he states, *"See then the goodness and the severity of God: towards them indeed that are fallen, the severity; but towards thee, the goodness of God, if thou abide in goodness, otherwise thou also shalt be cut off."* In Hebrews 10:26-27 we are told, *"For if we sin willfully after having the knowledge of the truth, there is now left no sacrifice for sins, But a certain dreadful expectation of judgment, and the rage of a fire which shall consume the adversaries."* In Peter 2:20-21 we read, *"For if, flying from the pollutions of the world, through the knowledge of our Lord and Saviour Jesus Christ, they be again entangled in them and overcome: their latter state is become unto them worse than the former. For it had been better for them not to have known the way of justice, than after they have known it, to turn back from that holy commandment which was delivered to them. For,*

---

[3] William A. Jurgens, "Commentaries on John," *The Faith of the Early Fathers* (Collegeville: The Liturgical Press), 202.

[4] Hippolytus, *Commentary on Proverbs (ante AD. 235).*

that of the true proverb has happened to them: The dog is returned to his vomit: and: The sow that was washed to her wallowing in the mire." And John tells us, *"For God so loved the world, as to give his only begotten Son: that whosoever believeth in him may not perish, but may have life everlasting."*[5] John does not say, "will not perish" and "will have eternal life," but rather "may," or in some translations "might have eternal life."

John Chrysostom, a Doctor of the Church, says it well when he preaches, *"'Is it enough,' saith one,' to believe on the Son, that one may have eternal life?' By no means. And hear Christ Himself declaring this, and saying, 'Not every one that saith unto Me, Lord, Lord, shall enter into the kingdom of heaven' (Mt 7:21); and the blasphemy against the Spirit is enough of itself to cast a man into hell. But why speak I of a portion of doctrine? Though a man believe rightly on the Father, the Son, and the Holy Ghost, yet if he lead not a right life, his faith will avail nothing towards his salvation."*[6]

There is no doubt that after accepting Jesus as our Savior; our salvation can still be lost. That is what Scripture tells us and that is what the Church teaches. Christ died so that our sins may be forgiven, with the key word being "may." If this were not the case, why would St. Paul have written so many letters to the early churches, warning them to renounce their sinful ways and to stand watch and be on guard? The

---

[5] Jn 3:16.
[6] John Chrysostom, *Homilies on John, 31:1 (AD. 391).*

church members he was addressing were all baptized and believed in Jesus as their Savior. St. Paul wrote these letters because he understood the power and devastation of sin and how it can alienate one from God.

By realizing how much our sins hurt and offend God, we are headed on the right road to heaven. But it is important to always remember that due to the temptations of Satan and his demons, combined with the weakness cast upon us by the sin of Adam (Original sin) and our inclination toward sin, the road to salvation is a long hard road. *"And a certain man said to him: Lord, are they few that are saved? But he said to them: Strive to enter by the narrow gate; for many, I say to you, shall seek to enter, and shall not be able"* (Lk 13: 23-24).

It is our choice in life to choose if we want to live our life in conformity with God's teachings or to live our life in sin. It is a hard road, and we must choose wisely on our journey if we are to find eternal happiness with God.

To connect to one's soul is to discover

one's humanity.

Chapter 5

WHAT CATHOLICS BELIEVE

What do Catholics believe? False answers to this question range from laughable misunderstandings of the Church's teachings to absurdities, depending on who is answering the question.

Many Christians of other denominations have little understanding of what the Catholic Church truly teaches and believes. Some tend to despise the Church for what they think the Church teaches. Many times these misunderstandings come from anti-Catholic writings filled with false and misguided explanations. Other times, misinformation comes from ex-Catholics or non-practicing Catholics who do not have a thorough understanding of the Church's teachings, for if they had, they would have never left the Church or stopped practicing their faith in the first place. I have discovered through life's experiences that it is best to understand what one is judging before making a judgment. Therefore, this chapter will be devoted to explaining some of the basic teachings of the Catholic faith.

The Catholic Church teaches that there is only one God. That God is timeless. He always has been and always will be. He is truth and love. God is the Father, the origin of everything, the Father of His children, the First Person of the Blessed Trinity, and that He is also almighty. His might is universal, and He is in charge of all things. Nothing is impossible when it comes to God. He is the creator of Heaven and earth.[1]

God made man to share in His blessed life. He calls man to seek Him, to know Him, to love Him with all his strength.[2] He made a covenant with Noah and Abraham. He sent his prophets to prepare man for the coming of the Savior. The Church believes that Holy Scriptures, even though written by man, were inspired by God and are truly His Word.

We as Catholics believe that God sent us Jesus Christ, His only Son, our Lord.[3] Scripture tells us, *"And the Word was made flesh and dwelt among us (and we saw his glory, the glory*

---

[1] Gen 1:1.
[2] CCC, 1.
[3] Gal 4:4-5, Mk 1:1.

as it were of the only begotten of the Father), full of grace and truth "(Jn 1:14). We also understand that Jesus is the Messiah, and that He is the fulfillment of the covenant that God made. The Greek translation of the Hebrew word "Messiah" is "Christ," which means the anointed. We read in Luke 2:11 that the angels told the shepherds, *"For, this day is born to you a Saviour, who is Christ the Lord, in the city of David."*

The Church teaches that Jesus was conceived of the Holy Spirit and born of the Virgin Mary. Jesus was conceived in the womb of the Virgin Mary by the power of the Holy Spirit without the seed of man. In Luke 1:26-35 we read,

And in the sixth month, the angel Gabriel was sent from God into a city of Galilee, called Nazareth, To a virgin espoused to a man whose name was Joseph, of the house of David: and the virgin's name was Mary. And the angel being come in, said unto her: Hail, full of grace, the Lord is with thee: blessed art thou among women. Who having heard, was troubled at his saying and thought with herself what manner of salutation this should be. And the angel said to her: Fear not, Mary, for thou hast found grace with God. Behold thou shalt conceive in thy womb and shalt bring forth a son: and thou shalt call his name Jesus. He shall be great and shall be called the Son of the most High. And the Lord God shall give unto him the throne of David his father: and he shall reign in the house of Jacob forever. And of his kingdom there shall be no end. And Mary said to the angel: How shall this be done, because I know not man? And the angel answering, said to her: The Holy Ghost shall come upon thee and the power of the Most High shall overshadow thee. And therefore also the Holy which shall be born of thee shall be called the Son of God.

The Church sees Jesus' virgin birth as a fulfillment of the promise made by God, given through the prophet Isaiah. In Matthew 1:19-23 we read,

Whereupon Joseph her husband, being a just man and not willing publicly to expose her, was minded to put her away privately. But while he thought on these things, behold the angel of the Lord appeared to him in his sleep, saying: Joseph, son of David, fear not to take unto thee Mary thy wife, for that which is conceived in her, is of the Holy Ghost. And she shall bring forth a son: and thou shalt call his name Jesus. For he shall save his people from their sins. Now all this was done that it might be fulfilled which the Lord spoke by the prophet, saying: Behold a virgin shall be with child, and bring forth a son: and they shall call his name Emmanuel, which being interpreted is, God with us.

Most of Jesus' private life is a mystery to us. His birth is revealed to us and is celebrated as Christmas. Jesus' early life is not recorded except for His presentation at the temple and the finding of Him when He was teaching at the temple at the age of twelve. Even much of Jesus' public life as a teacher is not covered in Scripture. Then His final days leading up to His death and resurrection are made known to us in Scripture and celebrated by the Church in the mystery of Easter. Why is this? Our fascination as humans in the daily activities of Jesus' life has nothing to do with God's message and instructions for our salvation and our understanding of Jesus as our Messiah and our Redeemer. Scripture tells us, "*Many other signs also did Jesus in the sight of his disciples, which are not written in this book. But these are written, that you may believe that Jesus is the Christ, the Son of God: and that believing, you may have life in his name.*"[4]

We know that Mary was betrothed to Joseph, who was a carpenter, and that Jesus learned the carpenter's trade. The beginning of Jesus' public life begins when John, the son of Zachariah, baptizes Jesus in the Jordan. We read in Mark 1:9-11, "*And it came to pass, in those days, Jesus came from Nazareth of Galilee and was baptized by John in the Jordan. And forthwith coming up out of the water, he saw the heavens opened and the Spirit as a dove descending and remaining on him. And there came a voice from heaven: Thou art my beloved Son; in*

---

[4] Jn 20:30-31.

thee I am well pleased." After Jesus' baptism, the Spirit guided Him out into the desert where He fasted for forty days and forty nights and was tempted by Satan.[5]

When Jesus returned from the desert, He began selecting His apostles and started preaching His Father's message.

> *From that time on Jesus began to preach and to say: Do penance, for the kingdom of heaven is at hand. And Jesus walking by the sea of Galilee, saw two brethren, Simon who is called Peter and Andrew his brother, casting a net into the sea (for they were fishermen). And he saith to them: Come ye after me, and I will make you to be fishers of men. And they immediately leaving their nets, followed him. And going on from thence, he saw other two brethren, James the son of Zebedee and John his brother, in a ship with Zebedee their father, mending their nets: and he called them. And they forthwith left their nets and father, and followed him* (Mt 4:17-22).

The Church teaches that Jesus chose Twelve Apostles to send forth and teach. They were Peter, Andrew, James, John, Philip, Bartholomew, Matthew, Thomas, James, Jude Simon, and Judas Iscariot.[6]

---

[5] Mt 4:1-2.
[6] Mt 10:3, Mk 3:16-19, Luke 6:14-16, Acts 1:13.

- Peter's original name was "Simon" or "Symeon," and he was renamed "Cephas" or "Petras" by Jesus. Peter was the first Pope and the head of the Roman Church. He was crucified upside-down in Rome.
- Andrew was Peter's brother. Andrew was crucified by the order of the Roman Governor of Patrae in Achaia. He was bound, rather than nailed, to the cross to prolong his suffering.[7]
- James the Greater was the son of Zebedee. James was beheaded by Herod Agrippa I.[8]
- John was also the son of Zebedee. John was the disciple whom Jesus loved and was the Evangelist.
- Philip was a native of Bethsaida on Lake Genesareth.
- Bartholomew is thought to have been beheaded or flayed alive and crucified, head downward in Albanopolis in Armenia.
- Matthew was also referred to as "Levi" and was an Evangelist.
- James the Less was also known also as "James the Just" or "James the Younger." He was the son of Alphaeus (Clophas) and is referred to in Scripture as "brother of the Lord." James the Less was an epistle writer and became the

---

[7] New Advent, "St. Andrew," *Catholic Encyclopedia*, http://www.newadvent.org/cathen/01471a.htm.
[8] Acts 12:1-2.

Bishop of the Jerusalem Church. He was clubbed to death.

- Jude, also known as "Thaddaeus," was the brother of James the Less and was an epistle writer. Jude and his brother James were relatives (cousins) of Jesus.
- Simon was also known as "Simon the Zealot" or "Simon the Canaanite." He died a martyr's death.
- Judas Iscariot was the apostle who betrayed Jesus and ended up committing suicide. After Jesus' death and resurrection, Matthias replaced Judas.

The Church believes that Jesus, on the first day of the Feast of Unleavened Bread, instituted the sacrament of the Eucharist at the Last Supper when He broke the bread, gave it to his disciples, and said, "Take this, all of you, and eat it; this is my body, which will be given up for you." When the supper was ended, He took the cup. Again He gave thanks and praise, gave the cup to his disciples, and said, "Take this, all of you, and drink from it; this is the cup of my blood, the blood of the new and everlasting covenant. It will be shed for you and for all so that sins may be forgiven. Do this in memory of me."[9]

After the Last Supper, Jesus retreated to a place called Gethsemane to pray. It is here that Judas Iscariot betrayed Jesus for the sum of thirty silver pieces.[10] In Matthew 26:47-49 we read, "*As he yet spoke, behold Judas, one of the*

---

[9] Lk 22:19-20.
[10] Mt 26:15.

twelve, came, and with him a great multitude with swords and clubs, sent from the chief priests and the ancients of the people. And he that betrayed him gave them a sign, saying: Whomsoever I shall kiss, that is he, hold him fast. And forthwith coming to Jesus, he said: Hail, Rabbi. And he kissed him." Jesus was arrested and would suffer immensely till His death. He was slapped and struck. People spat in His face and ridiculed Him.[11] He was then handed over to Pilate, the Roman governor who ordered Him severely scourged and then crucified. Catholics believe that He was crucified for our sake. Mark 15:1-15 tells us,

And straightway in the morning, the chief priests holding a consultation with the ancients and the scribes and the whole council, binding Jesus, led him away, and delivered him to Pilate. And Pilate asked him: Art thou the king of the Jews? But he answering, saith to him: Thou sayest it. And the chief priests accused him in many things. And Pilate again asked him, saying: Answerest thou nothing? Behold in how many things they accuse thee. But Jesus still answered nothing: so that Pilate wondered. Now on the festival day he was wont to release unto them one of the prisoners, whomsoever they demanded. And there was one called Barabbas, who was put in prison with some seditious men, who in the sedition had committed

---

[11] Mt 26:67.

murder. And when the multitude was come up, they began to desire that he would do as he had ever done unto them. And Pilate answered them and said: Will you that I release to you the king of the Jews? For he knew that the chief priests had delivered him up out of envy. But the chief priests moved the people, that he should rather release Barabbas to them. And Pilate again answering, saith to them: What will you then that I do to the king of the Jews? But they again cried out: Crucify him. And Pilate saith to them: Why, what evil hath he done? But they cried out the more: Crucify him. And so Pilate being willing to satisfy the people, released to them Barabbas: and delivered up Jesus, when he had scourged him, to be crucified.

The Church reinforces what Tradition and Scripture teach us: Jesus rose from the dead on the third day in fulfillment of the Scriptures.

And at the end of the sabbath, when it began to dawn towards the first day of the week, came Mary Magdalen and the other Mary, to see the sepulchre. And behold there was a great earthquake. For an angel of the Lord descended from heaven and coming rolled back the stone and sat upon it. And his countenance was as lightning and his raiment as snow. And for fear of him, the guards were struck with terror and became as dead men. And the angel answering, said to the women: Fear not you; for I know that you seek Jesus who was crucified. He is not here. For he is risen, as he said. Come, and see the place where the Lord was laid. And going quickly, tell ye his disciples that he is risen. And behold he will go before you into Galilee. There you shall see him. Lo, I have foretold it to you. And they went out quickly from the sepulchre with fear and great joy, running to tell his disciples. And behold, Jesus met them, saying: All hail. But they came up and took hold of his feet and adored him. Then Jesus said to them: Fear not. Go, tell my brethren that they go into Galilee. There they shall see me (Mt 28:1-10).

Jesus appeared to all the apostles, plus hundreds more of His followers, so that they would believe that He indeed was the Son of God. He commissioned the apostles to *"Go therefore, teach ye all nations: baptizing them in the name of the Father and of the Son and of the Holy Ghost, teaching them to observe all that I have commanded you"* (Mt 28:19-20).

The Church teaches that Jesus ascended into Heaven and took His seat at the right hand of God.[12] He will come again in glory to judge the living and the dead, and His kingdom will have no end.

The Church believes in the Holy Spirit, who is the Third Person of the Blessed Trinity. Even

---

[12] Mk 16:19, Lk 24:51, Acts 1.

though the Holy Spirit is really distinct, as a Person, from the Father and the Son, He is consubstantial (of the same substance) with Them, being God like Them, He possesses with Them one and the same Divine Essence or Nature. He proceeds, not by way of generation, but by way of spiration, from the Father and the Son together as from a single principle.[13]

The Holy Spirit along with the Father and the Son are to be adored and glorified. The Church teaches that the Holy Spirit guided the apostles in their preaching (Sacred Traditions) and writing (Sacred Scripture) of Jesus' teachings and that "Sacred Tradition and Sacred Scripture make up a single sacred deposit of the Word of God."[14]

How do we know that the Catholic Church is the one true Church? There are four marks used to identify the Church that Jesus started. The Church is one, holy, catholic, and apostolic. There can only be one true Church that Jesus started. He did not develop one Church for the Jews and another for the Gentiles. In Rom 12:5 we read, *"So we being many, are one body in Christ."* This body is referring to his Church. We read this again in 1 Cor 12:13, *"For in one Spirit were we all baptized into one body, whether Jews or Gentiles, whether bond or free: and in one Spirit we have all been made to drink."* How do we know that the Catholic Church is one? The Catholic Church is one because its mem-

---

[13] New Advent, "Holy Ghost," *Catholic Encyclopedia*, http://www.newadvent.org/cathen/07409a.htm.
[14] CCC, 97.

bers profess their unity in the same beliefs. They accept and believe in the doctrine and morals that Jesus and the apostles taught. Catholics participate in the same Mass with the same sacraments and have only one person, the Pope, as their visible leader. Every hour, throughout the day, somewhere in the world the Catholic Mass is being said. It may be spoken in a different language, but it is the same Mass.

How do we know that the Catholic Church is holy? Jesus makes the Church holy by His grace. In Ephesians 5:25-27, we're taught, *"Christ also loved the church, and delivered himself up for it: That he might sanctify it, cleansing it by the laver of water in the word of life: That he might present it to himself, a glorious church, not having spot or wrinkle, or any such thing; but that it should be holy and without blemish."* The Church teaches the same Holy doctrine that Jesus and the apostles taught, giving its members a means to living a holy life. This does not mean that all its members will go to Heaven, for Jesus warns us, *"Not everyone that saith to me, Lord, Lord, shall enter into the kingdom of heaven: but he that doth the will of my Father who is in heaven, he shall enter into the kingdom of heaven. Many will say to me in that day: Lord, Lord, have not we prophesied in thy name and cast out devils in thy name and done many miracles in thy name? And then will I profess unto them: I never knew you. Depart from me, you that work iniquity"* (Mt 7:21-23).

We as humans all have free will, and in God's mercy and perfect justice, He has given us the choice to choose a life of holiness and with it receive the reward of Heaven or to choose a life of sinfulness, turning our backs on God's teachings and reaping eternal punishment in Hell.

The third mark of the true Church is that it must be catholic. "Catholic" in Greek means universal, meaning that Jesus' Church was established for everyone on earth. He told the apostles, *"Go therefore, teach ye all nation."* At the same time Jesus also promised to be with His Church till the end of time, saying, *"And behold I am with you all days, even to the consummation of the world"* (Mt 28:19-20). To prove that the Church Jesus started was called the Catholic Church in its infancy, we can read a letter written by Ignatius of Antioch to the Smyrnaeans in AD 110 in which he states, *"Wherever the bishop appears, let the people be there; just as wherever Jesus Christ is, there is the Catholic Church."* There are several other early writings using the words "Catholic Church." A few of them are *The Martyrdom of Polycarp* written in AD 155, *The Muratorian Canon* AD 177, and the *Demurrer Against the Heretics* written by Tertullian in AD 200. The Catholic Church today can be found throughout the world teaching the same doctrine that Christ taught His apostles, and its teachings have been uninterrupted since its establishment on Pentecost Sunday.

The fourth and final mark that Christ's Church must have is that it is apostolic. The Catholic Church contains the mark of being apostolic because Jesus commissioned the first leaders of His Church, the apostles, to go forth and preach His teachings to all. He chose Peter as the first Pope; the apostles were the first bishops.[15] This apostolic succession of the Bishops of Rome has been unbroken throughout the Church's existence, proving that the Catholic Church is truly apostolic.

Every Sunday at Mass during the profession of faith, Catholics recite, *"We acknowledge one Baptism for the forgiveness of sins.* In John 3:5 we read, *"Jesus answered: Amen, amen, I say to thee, unless a man be born again of water and the Holy Ghost, he cannot enter into the kingdom of God."* We're told in Acts 2:38 that Baptism forgives our sins and gives us grace: *"Peter said to them: Do penance: and be baptized every one of you in the name of Jesus Christ, for the remission of your sins. And you shall receive the gift of the Holy Ghost."* There are several other passages in Scripture that tell of the spiritual effect that is received from the sacrament of Baptism.[16]

In my discussions about Baptism, I often hear the question, "What about all the people who have never heard the Gospels of Jesus proclaimed? Are they doomed to Hell?" The Church teaches that there are two other kinds of Baptism. One is called a Baptism of desire. The Catholic *Catechism* tells us, *"For catechumens who die before their Baptism, their explicit desire to receive it, together with repentance for their sins, and charity, assures them the salvation that they were not able to receive through the sacra-*

---

[15] Mt 16:18-19.
[16] Acts 2:38, 22:16; Rom 6:1–4; 1 Cor 6:11, 12:13; Gal 3:26–27; Eph 5:25-27; Col 2:11–12; Titus 3:5; 1 Pet 3:18–22.

ment." It goes on to say, "*Every man who is igno-rant of the Gospel of Christ and of his Church, but seeks the truth and does the will of God in accordance with his understanding of it, can be saved. It may be supposed that such persons would have desired Baptism explicitly if they had known its necessity.*"[17] The other type of Baptism is called the Baptism of blood. This takes place when someone accepts death for the sake of the faith without having previously been baptized. Through this martyrdom, they are baptized by their death for and with Christ.[18]

In the profession of faith, we continue to say, "*We look for the resurrection of the dead, and the life of the world to come. Amen.*" Catholics believe in the resurrection of the dead not only as a spiritual resurrection but also as a bodily resurrection. In John 5:28 we read, "*Wonder not at this: for the hour cometh, wherein all that are in the graves shall hear the voice of the Son of God. And they that have done good things shall come forth unto the resurrection of life: but they that have done evil, unto the resurrection of judgment.*" When this day comes and our bodies are resurrected, they will not be as our bodies are now but will be glorified bodies. When Christ rose from the dead, He did not return in His earthly body to an earthly way of life. He returned in a glorified body to a spiritual life. This explains why the apostles on the road to Emmaus did not recognize Jesus until He broke the bread with them. It was not in His physical

---

[17] CCC, 1259-1260.
[18] Ibid, 1258.

appearance but in this breaking and blessing of the bread that they recognized Him.[19] Paul tells us, *"Behold, I tell you a mystery. We shall all indeed rise again: but we shall not all be changed. In a moment, in the twinkling of an eye, at the last trumpet: for the trumpet shall sound and the dead shall rise again incorruptible. And we shall be changed. For this corruptible must put on incorruption: and this mortal must put on immortality"* (1 Cor 15:51-53).

What does it mean when Catholics say, *"and the life of the world to come?"* They believe that after the final judgment, God will fulfill His promise of remaking the universe with new Heavens and a new earth.[20] In this new world, God will dwell amongst them and no longer will there be pain, suffering, or death.[21] The faithful will have received God's reward of eternal life and happiness.

---

[19] Lk 24:13-35.
[20] 2 Peter 3:13.
[21] Rev 21:3-4.

Chapter 6

THE EUCHARIST

The Eucharist is one of the most important yet misunderstood gifts that God has given us through his Son Jesus Christ. "Eucharist" comes from the Greek word *eucharistia*, which means thanksgiving. It is the name given to the Blessed Sacrament of the altar. The Eucharist has three entities: as a sacrament, as a sacrifice, and as the real presence of the body and blood of Christ.[1]

---

[1] J. Pohle, "Eucharist," *The Catholic Encyclopedia*, Volume V (Robert Appleton Company, 1909).

IN SEARCH OF TRUTH

When Jesus preaches in the Synagogue in Capernaum he says,

> *I am the bread of life. Your fathers did eat manna in the desert: and are dead. This is the bread which cometh down from heaven: that if any man eat of it, he may not die. I am the living bread which came down from heaven. If any man eat of this bread, he shall live forever: and the bread that I will give is my flesh, for the life of the world. The Jews therefore strove among themselves, saying: How can this man give us his flesh to eat? Then Jesus said to them: Amen, amen, I say unto you: except you eat the flesh of the Son of man and drink his blood, you shall not have life in you. He that eateth my flesh and drinketh my blood hath everlasting life: and I will raise him up in the last day. For my flesh is meat indeed: and my blood is drink indeed. He that eateth my flesh and drinketh my blood, abideth in me: and I in him. As the living Father hath sent me and I live by the Father: so he that eateth me, the same also shall live by me. This is the bread that came down from heaven. Not as your fathers did eat manna and are dead. He that eateth this bread shall live for ever* (Jn 6:48-59).

This was God's future promise of His Real Presence in the Eucharist, which would be instituted at the Last Supper. We know this was taken literally by the Jews due to their quarreling, and many of the disciples, unable to understand literally the eating of His flesh, ended up leaving.

> *But Jesus, knowing in himself that his disciples murmured at this, said to them: Doth this scandalize you? If then you shall see the Son of man ascend up where he was before? It is the spirit that quickeneth: the flesh profiteth nothing. The words that I have spoken to you are spirit and life. But there are some of you that believe not. For Jesus knew from the beginning who they were that did not believe and who he was that would betray him. And he said: Therefore did I say to you that no man can come to me, unless it be given him by my Father. After this, many of his disciples went back and walked no more with him* (Jn 6:62-67).

At the Last Supper, Jesus established the sacrament of the Eucharist. *"And whilst they were at supper, Jesus took bread and blessed and broke and gave to his disciples, and said: Take ye and eat. This is my body. And taking the chalice, he gave thanks and gave to them, saying: Drink ye all of this. For this is my blood of the new testament, which shall be shed for many unto remission of sins"* (Mt 26:26-28). The apostles understood that "this is my body" and "take ye, and eat" were to be taken literally and were the fulfillment of what Jesus had preached earlier at Capernaum.

The apostles and the early Church believed Jesus consecrated the bread and wine and transformed it into His body and blood. This miracle was repeated in what was to become known as the Mass. In 1 Corinthians 11:26-30, the true presence is made known when Paul writes, *"For as often as you shall eat this bread and drink the chalice, you shall shew (proclaim) the death of the Lord, until he come. Therefore, whosoever shall eat this bread, or drink the chalice of the Lord unworthily, shall be guilty of the body and of the blood of the Lord. But let a man prove himself: and so let him eat of that bread and drink of the chalice. For he that eateth and drinketh unworthily eateth and drinketh judgment to himself, not discerning the body of the Lord."* If the bread and wine weren't truly the body and blood of our Lord Jesus Christ, how would we be committing an offense against it by receiving it in a sinful state?

If we meditate on this passage, we will come to realize how damaging it is to our spiritual lives to receive the Eucharist with grievous sin on our souls. As the young priest (mentioned in the Introduction) preached, "The Communion lines are long but the lines for Confession (Reconciliation) are short." Was he right when he said this indicated that most people think sin no longer matters? God is telling us that it *does* matter. Let us not approach the sacrament of the Eucharist with grievous sin on our souls, for as Paul tells us, we are bringing judgment on ourselves.

There are Catholics who do not believe in the Real Presence of Christ's body and blood, and by watching the lack of reverence of many who receive communion, I wonder what their true beliefs are. Their refusal to accept this teaching is extremely serious, for the Church teaches infallibly that Christ is present in the Eucharist through transubstantiation. People will question, "If it is really the flesh and blood of Jesus, why doesn't it look, feel, and taste like flesh and blood? Also, why does one who is allergic to wheat have an allergic reaction when he or she receives the Eucharist?" By understanding the definition of transubstantiation, they should not have these doubts.

Because this is a layman's guide, I'm going to give a simple explanation of transubstantiation. If you have a hard time understanding this explanation, I would recommend that you do further research and reading on the subject. The Eucharist is one of the greatest gifts the Lord has given us, and once you understand that it is truly the body and blood of our Lord Jesus, your respect for the Eucharist will change.

To understand transubstantiation, one must understand a little philosophy and at least two words: "accidents and substance." Accidents are what the senses perceive, such as taste, color, aroma, shape, and other physical properties. Substance is the invisible, intangible, interior reality of a person or object, the essence of its nature. Substance cannot be seen, smelled, or tasted. During the consecration, the substance of the bread and wine, its interior reality, is transformed into the substance of the body and blood of Jesus Christ. Due to the miracle of the Eucharist, the accidents of the bread and wine remain unchanged; thus, the smell, look, and taste remain the same even though the substance has changed.

The Council of Trent says, and the *Catechism of the Catholic Church* repeats, *"by the consecration of the bread and wine there takes place a change of the whole substance of the bread into the substance of the body of Christ our Lord and of the whole substance of the wine into the substance of his blood."*[2] This changing of the substance and not of the accidents explains why the Eucharist still appears and tastes like bread and wine even though it has become the body and blood of Jesus.

It is natural to have a hard time believing and accepting a teaching that the Lord taught us when we do not fully understand. It is our human nature to try to use our reason and logic to understand, but sometimes these are not enough. St. John Chrysostom (AD 347-407), one of the great Doctors of the church, says, *"Let us submit to God in all things and not contradict Him, even if what He says seems contrary to our reason and intellect; rather let His words prevail over our reason and intellect. Let us act in this way with regard to the (eucharistic) mysteries, looking not only at what falls under our senses but holding on to His words. For His word cannot lead us astray."*[3]

Let's look at what the early Fathers of the Church say concerning their belief that the Eucharist contains the Real Presence of Christ's body and blood in the sacrament of the altar. St. Ignatius of Antioch writes, *"The Eucharist is that*

---

[2] John Young, "Transubstantiation and Reason," (Catholic Information Center on the Internet, 1998).
[3] St. John Chrysostom, *Homily on Matthew*, 82.4; PG 58.743.

flesh of Our Savior Jesus Christ who suffered for our sins and whom the Father in His loving kindness raised again."[4] Justin Martyr preaches, *"For not as common bread nor common drink do we receive these; but since Jesus Christ our Savior was made incarnate by the word of God and had both flesh and blood for our salvation, so too, as we have been taught, the food which has been made into the Eucharist by the Eucharistic prayer set down by him, and by the change of which our blood and flesh is nurtured, is both the flesh and the blood of that incarnated Jesus."[5]* St. Cyril of Alexandria conveys the same message while preaching on the mysteries of the faith: *"That which seems to be bread, is not bread, though it tastes like it, but the Body of Christ, and that which seems to be wine, is not wine, though it too tastes as such, but the Blood of Christ ... draw inner strength by receiving this bread as spiritual food and your soul will rejoice."[6]* St. John Chrysostom states, *"It is not the power of man which makes what is put before us the Body and Blood of Christ, but the power of Christ Himself who was crucified for us. The priest standing there in the place of Christ says these words but their power and grace are from God. 'This is My Body,' he says, and these words transform what lies before him."* [7]

---

[4] St. Ignatius, *Epistle to the Smyrnians*, 7,1, PG 5. 714.

[5] Justin Martyr, *The First Apology of Justin*, 66 (AD 110-165).

[6] St. Cyril of Alexandria, *Catecheses*, 22, 9, (Myst.) 4, P.G. 33, 1103

[7] Chrysostom, *Homily on Judas' Betrayal*, 1.6: PG 49.380; cf. *Homily on Matthew* 82.5: PG 58.744.

In summary, I will use a quote from Theodore of Mopsueta, a faithful witness to the faith of the Church: *"The Lord did not say: This is a symbol of My Body, and this a symbol of My Blood but: 'This is My Body and My Blood.' He teaches us not to look to the nature of those things which lie before us and are perceived by the senses, for by the prayer of thanksgiving and the words spoken over them, they have been changed into Flesh and Blood."*[8,9]

---

[8] Theodore of Mopsuestia, *Commentary on Matthew*, c. 26; PG 66.714

[9] Quotations in footnotes 3, 4, and 6-8 can be found in Pope Paul VI, Encyclical Letter "Mysterium Fidei" (Mystery of Faith), Sept. 3, 1965.

Chapter 7

WHY PURGATORY EXISTS

To understand the concept of Purgatory, we must remember that in order to enter Heaven, we need to be purified of all stain of sin committed during our lives. Scripture tells us there can be no evil in Heaven: *"There shall not enter into it anything defiled"* (Rev 21:27).

So what exactly is Purgatory? Purgatory is a temporary state of purification where the soul is sent to remove all uncleanliness and stain from sin so that it may enter Heaven. We might think that once the soul is sent to Purgatory, it would be happy knowing that it was not condemned to Hell and would eventually get to Heaven. This is not the case, though, because once the soul has been given a glimpse of how great God is, it suffers immensely from having to be separated from Him. This burning desire to return to God's presence is greater suffering than any known to man. What makes matters worse is there is nothing that the soul can do while in Purgatory to help his or her plight. Unlike the living, who can perform works of charity, almsgiving, fasting, and penance for their sins, the souls in Purgatory are unable to do so. This is one of the reasons why we should pray for the souls in Purgatory. When I pray for the release of souls from Purgatory, I also ask that when they are released to Heaven, they will remember me and pray for my soul.

Many Christians do not understand that we have two judgments for our sins. The first, or particular, judgment occurs at death when we receive our just reward or the punishment for how we've lived. *"And as it is appointed unto men once to die, and after this the judgment: So also Christ was offered once to exhaust the sins of many. The second time he shall appear without sin to them that expect him unto salvation"* (Heb 9:27-28). In Luke we read," *And one of those robbers who were hanged blasphemed him, saying: If thou be Christ, save thyself and us. But the other answering, rebuked him, saying: Neither dost thou fear God, seeing thou art condemned under the same condemnation? And we indeed justly: for we receive the due reward of our deeds. But this man hath done no evil. And he said to Jesus: Lord, remember me when thou shalt come into thy kingdom. And Jesus said to him: Amen I say to thee: This day thou shalt be with me in paradise"* (Lk 23:39-43). These passages confirm that we do not have to wait till the second coming for our reward or punishment. We will know immediately after death if we will enter into Heaven or worse, if we will be sentenced to Hell or to Purgatory to cleanse our soul of the stain left by our sins.[1]

The second judgment will come at the end of the world. *"And when the Son of man shall come in his majesty, and all the angels with him, then shall he sit upon the seat of his majesty. And all nations shall be gathered together before him: and he shall separate them one from another, as the shepherd separateth the sheep from the goats"* (Mt 25:31-32). This is called the general (final) judgment day in which as Scripture tells us, all man's sins will be made known. *"For there is nothing covered that shall not be revealed: nor hidden that shall not be known"* (Lk 12:2). After the final judgment, there will no longer be a need for Purgatory, and it will cease to exist.

Let's look at what Scripture tells us about praying for the dead.

So Judas [Maccabeus], having gathered together his army, came into the city Odollam: and when the seventh day came, they purified themselves according to the custom and kept the sabbath in the same place. And the day following, Judas came with his company to take away the bodies

---

[1] CCC, 1021.

of them that were slain and to bury them with their kinsmen in the sepulchres of their fathers. And they found under the coats of the slain some of the donaries of the idols of Jamnia, which the law forbiddeth the Jews: so that all plainly saw, for this cause they were slain. Then they all blessed the just judgment of the Lord, who had discovered the things that were hidden. And so betaking themselves to prayers they besought him that the sin which had been committed might be forgotten. But the most valiant Judas exhorted the people to keep themselves from sin, forasmuch as they saw before their eyes what had happened because of the sins of those that were slain. And making a gathering, he sent twelve thousand drachms of silver to Jerusalem for sacrifice to be offered for the sins of the dead, thinking well and religiously concerning the resurrection, (For if he had not hoped that they that were slain should rise again, it would have seemed superfluous and vain to pray for the dead,) And because he considered that the who had fallen asleep with godliness had great grace laid up for them. It is therefore a holy and wholesome thought to pray for the dead, that they may be loosed from sins (2 Macc 12: 38-46).

We know that once a soul enters Heaven it is not in need of prayers, and once a soul enters Hell, no amount of prayer will get it released. So I ask "Why would Judas be praying and making atonement for the soldiers' sin of wearing the amulets if indeed it did not help?" If prayer could not affect the condition of a dead man's soul, why would Judas bother? This Scripture proves that it was customary for the Old Testament Jews to pray for the dead and that for the first fifteen hundred years Christians accepted this custom without question.

The Maccabees Scripture about praying for the dead is one of the main reasons why the Protestant reformers choose to disregard the two books of Maccabees; the books countered what the reformers were trying to teach. Rather than to seek understanding of the Traditions and writings, they chose to ignore truth and reject Scripture.

Let's look at what some of the early Christians said about Purgatory. Origen (AD 185-232) writes,

> *If a man departs this life with lighter faults, he is condemned to fire which burns away the lighter materials, and prepares the soul for the kingdom of God, where nothing defiled may enter.... It remains then that you be committed to the fire, which will burn the light materials; for our God to those who can comprehend heavenly things is called a cleansing fire. But this fire consumes not the creature, but what the creature has himself built, wood, and hay and stubble. It is manifest that the fire destroys the wood of our*

> *transgressions and then returns to us the reward of our great works.*[2]

St. John Chrysostom preaches, *"Let us help and commemorate them. If Job's sons were purified by their father's sacrifice (Job 1:5), why would we doubt that our offerings for the dead bring them some consolation? Let us not hesitate to help those who have died and to offer our prayers for them."*[3] Saint Augustine writes in his book *The City of God*, *"Temporal punishments are suffered by some in this life only, by some after death, by some both here and hereafter, but all of them before that last and strictest judgment. But not all who suffer temporal punishments after death will come to eternal punishments, which are to follow after that judgment."*[4]

The history of early Christianity shows that Christians of the first few centuries were not shy about questioning any changes in beliefs that were different from what was passed down to them from their ancestors. There is no such historical record of questioning or rejecting Purgatory in the early years of the Church.[5]

Let's look at why there must be a Purgatory. We agree that God is all good. Evil is the absence of good; therefore, there can be no evil in Heaven. Man is not all good and has the tendency to be weak and commit sins due to the effects of the sin of Adam. Even though man

---

[2] *Patres Groeci*, XIII, col. 445, 448.

[3] John Chrysostom, *Homilies on First Corinthians*, 41:5.

[4] St. Augustine, *The City of God*, 21:13.

[5] Karl Keating, *Catholicism and Fundamentalism*, (San Francisco: Ignatius, 1988), 192.

sins, all sins are not equal. Some sins are worse than others. A person dying with a deadly sin on his or her soul, without repentance, is truly spiritually dead. *"He that knoweth his brother to sin a sin which is not to death, let him ask: and life shall be given to him, who sinneth not to death. There is a sin unto death. For that I say not that any man ask"* (1 Jn 5:16).

We understand that there has to be a spiritual place besides Heaven and Hell. 1 Peter 4:6 states, *".... for this cause was the Gospel preached also to the dead: That they might be judged indeed according to men, in the flesh: but may live according to God, in the Spirit."* We know that once a soul is sent to Hell, it is there for eternity. We also know that before Jesus' death and resurrection a soul could not get to Heaven, so where were the souls of the dead who lived holy lives?

If we look at the common man, we see that he lives his life in a casual or nonchalant manner when it comes to God. We would hope that this manner would not condemn him to Hell, yet at the same time we understand that in God's justice it would not merit immediate entrance into the heavenly kingdom with the Communion of Saints.

Another reason why there must be a Purgatory is that when people die and their souls leave this physical world to stand before God for their first judgment, only then do their souls comprehend how bad and evil the effects of their lives' sins truly are. Their souls realize how greatly these sinful acts have offended God and understand how unworthy and unfit they are to enter the Lord's presence. Realizing their un-worthiness to go to Heaven, the souls will want to cleanse themselves to make them worthy to enter. I compare this to a bride on her wedding day. She goes out and purchases a fancy wedding dress along with new shoes and undergarments. She has her hair styled and makeup done so she will look more beautiful than she has ever looked in preparation for her bride-groom. Souls, once realizing how beautiful and great God is, will want to do the same.

The New Testament's Letter to the Hebrews states, *"But you are come to Mount Sion and to the city of the living God, the heavenly Jerusalem, and to the company of many thousands of angels, And to the church of the firstborn who are written in the heavens, and to God the judge of all, and to the spirits (souls) of the just made perfect"* (Heb 12:22-23).

How will the soul be cleansed of all stain of sin and be made perfect? One means of purification is through the burning desire that the soul will have after receiving a glimpse of how magnificent and loving God truly is. In 1 Corinthians 3:15 we read. *"If any man's work burn, he shall suffer loss; but he himself shall be saved, yet so as by fire."* The soul will feel pain like it has never felt before. We all know how hard it is on earth to be separated from our loved ones and how, after a long separation, we long to be reunited with them. How much worse will suffering be for our souls when they catch a glimpse of the wonders of God, which are unfathomable to man? Seeing God's wonder, and at the same time realizing that God had sent His own Son to teach us how to live our lives and how we failed to follow his Son's teachings, will bring our souls much regret. This realization of His great love and our lack of it will cause much grief and shame. This grief and shame will add to the immense suffering that our souls would already suffer due to their separation from their loved one (God).

This burning desire for union with God can be looked on as a purgation of fire, which helps cleanse the soul like a cleansing fire. In Daniel 12:10 we read, *"Many shall be chosen and made white and shall be tried as fire: and the wicked shall deal wickedly. And none of the wicked shall understand: but the learned shall understand."* The prophecy of Zechariah tells us, *"And I will bring the third part through the fire and will refine them as silver is refined: and I will try them as gold is tried. They shall call on my name, and I will hear them. I will say: Thou art my people. And they shall say: The Lord is my God"* (Zch 13:9). This theme is repeated again in Malachi 3:2-3.

The second way to help cleanse the evil from the soul is through the intercessory powers of the Blessed Mother and the saints in Heaven. With their prayers and intercessions, great deliverance from this suffering can be accomplished.

The third way is for people on earth to pray for the souls in Purgatory. Individual and group prayer services are good. What better way to please God than to have a Mass (the suffering of the Son of God) offered up in one's name asking for their deliverance from Purgatory? By praying for the dead, we are performing a selfless, charitable act, which cannot be considered anything but good in the eyes of God. We are not only helping the souls in Purgatory but are helping ourselves achieve a closer union with God through this act of love and charity.

Chapter 8

A BASIC GUIDE TO THE CELEBRATION OF THE MASS

The cornerstone of Catholic worship is the celebration of the Eucharist, commonly known as the Mass. The term "Eucharist" means giving thanks. In the early Church, this celebration was also known as the Lord's Supper, the breaking of the bread, and the liturgy.

What exactly is the Mass? The Catholic Church considers the Mass a true and proper sacrifice to God.[1] To a non-Catholic attending

---

[1] *Council of Trent*, Sess. XXII, can. 1.

Mass for the first time, the Mass may seem very ritualistic with the various postures of standing, sitting, and kneeling. To a point, that is correct. But as I break down and explain the different parts of the Mass, I hope that your understanding of why Catholics worship as they do will become clearer, and that the beauty of the sacrifice of the Mass will be seen and understood.

The Mass can be divided into two parts of worship called the Liturgy of the Word and the Liturgy of the Eucharist. These two liturgies, combined with the Introductory Rites, which precede the Liturgy of the Word, and the Concluding Rites, which follow the Liturgy of the Eucharist, constitute the Mass.

INTRODUCTORY RITES

The beginning of the Mass is called the Gathering, during which members of the congregation enter the church and find a place to sit. Upon entering the church, we kneel and silently pray a few individual prayers in preparation for the Mass.

Entrance Procession: When it is time for Mass to begin, the commentator will ask for everyone to *"please rise"* (stand). An entrance Antiphon, or opening song, is normally sung as the priest and other ministers proceed to the altar. The priest, upon arriving at the altar, will show reverence to it by bowing and kissing the altar. On solemn occasions, he may also incense it.

Greeting: The priest begins the greeting by praying, *"In the name of the Father, and of the Son, and of the Holy Spirit,"* while making the sign of the cross. All present will make the sign of the cross and respond, **"Amen."** This shows our Christian belief in the Blessed Trinity. The priest then greets the congregation in the Lord's name, using one of the greetings from the missal (official prayer book), such as, **"The grace of our Lord Jesus Christ and the love of God and the communion of the Holy Spirit be with you all."** The congregation responds, **"And with your spirit."** At this point, the priest may make a brief statement about the feast day or Mass that is being celebrated.

Penitential Rite: The priest next recites, **"Brethren (Brothers and sisters), let us acknowledge our sins, and so prepare ourselves to celebrate the sacred mysteries."** This statement is followed by a brief moment of reflection. After bringing to mind our sins, the whole congregation then recites one of the three forms of the Penitential Rite. The first and most common form is the prayer known as the Confiteor. In the Confiteor, we admit that we have sinned against God. We ask for the Blessed Mother and all the saints to pray to the Lord our God on our behalf:

> **"I confess to almighty God,**
> **and to you, my brothers and sisters,**
> **that I have greatly sinned,**
> **in my thoughts and in my words,**
> **in what I have done,**
> **and in what I have failed to do;**
> **through my fault, through my fault,**
> **through my most grievous fault;**

> **therefore I ask blessed Mary, ever Virgin,**
> **all the Angels and Saints,**
> **and you, my brothers and sisters,**
> **to pray for me to the Lord, our God."**

The priest then prays, **"May almighty God have mercy on us, forgive us our sins, and bring us to everlasting life."** And everyone will respond, **"Amen."** The Penitential Rite, combined with the reception of the Eucharist, grants us forgiveness for venial (lesser) sins if we are truly sorry.[2] During the Easter season or special occasions, the Rite of Blessing and Sprinkling Holy Water may replace the customary Penitential Rite.

Kyrie (Lord Have Mercy): The next acclamation is known as the Kyrie. It is either sung or recited in English or in Greek:

> Priest: **"Lord, have mercy."**   All: **"Lord, have mercy."**
> Priest: **"Christ, have mercy."** All: **"Christ, have mercy."**
> Priest: **"Lord, have mercy**.**"**   All: **"Lord, have mercy**.**"**
>
> Priest: **"Kyrie, eleison."**   All: **"Kyrie, eleison."**
> Priest: **"Christe, eleison."** All: **"Christe, eleison."**
> Priest: **"Kyrie, eleison."**   All: **"Kyrie, eleison."**

---

[2] CCC, 1394, 1416.

Gloria: When the Kyrie is finished, it is time to praise God by singing or reciting the ancient hymn called the Gloria.[3] The Gloria starts out by repeating what the angels said to the shepherds in Luke's narrative of the birth of Christ: "Glory to God in the highest, and on earth peace to people of good will" (Lk 2:13-14). Several acclamations of praise and supplications for mercy follow, and the prayer finishes with stating our belief in the Holy Trinity.

The priest may begin the Gloria by inviting the congregation to join in praising God:

> **"Glory to God in the highest,
> and on earth peace to people of good will.
> We praise you, we bless you, we adore you, we glorify you, we give you thanks for your great glory, Lord God, heavenly King, O God, almighty Father.
> Lord Jesus Christ, Only Begotten Son,
> Lord God, Lamb of God,
> Son of the Father,
> you take away the sins of the world, have mercy on us;
> you take away the sins of the world, receive our prayer;
> you are seated at the right hand of the Father, have mercy on us.
> For you alone are the Holy One,
> you alone are the Lord,
> you alone are the Most High, Jesus Christ, with the Holy Spirit,
> in the glory of God the Father. Amen."**

---

[3] During Advent and Lent, the Gloria is left out.

The Opening Prayer: The opening prayer changes frequently. The priest will say, **"Let us pray."** There is a moment of silence for everyone to personally pray, after which the priest "collects" all our prayers into one by praying out loud on behalf of the congregation. At the prayer's conclusion, everyone responds, **"Amen."** This concludes the Introductory Rites, and everyone sits in preparation for the beginning of the Liturgy of the Word.

LITURGY OF THE WORD

The Liturgy of the Word is the first major part of the Mass. It begins after the Opening Prayer and is the part of the Mass when the Word of God is read and explained.

First Reading: The Liturgy of the Word begins with the reader (lector) proclaiming, **"A reading from the book of ..."** The First Reading changes daily throughout the Church year and usually come from the Old Testament (Jewish Scriptures), which were written to prepare the world for the coming of our Savior. When the reading is finished, the lector proclaims, **"The Word of the Lord,"** to which the congregation responds: **"Thanks be to God."**

Responsorial Psalm: The choir or cantor will first sing or recite the response to let the congregation know how the response goes, and then the congregation will repeat it. Then the choir or cantor will sing or recite a psalm as the congregation joins in the response. The psalms come from the book of Psalms located in the Old Testament. The singing of and memorization of the Psalms has been throughout Judeo-Christian history a highly favored way of praising, giving thanks to, and worshipping God.

Second Reading: The Second Reading is read only on Sundays and major feast days. The lector will begin by proclaiming, **"A reading from the Letter of ..., or Acts ..."** The Second Reading comes from the New Testament letters attributed to Paul, James, Peter, John, and Jude and writings from the Book of Acts, written by the Gospel writer Luke. These letters were written by Jesus' disciples to the early Church to give them direction in understanding God's message, which was taught through the teachings of His Son, Jesus. When the reading is finished the lector proclaims, **"The word of the Lord."** The congregation responds, **"Thanks be to God."**

Gospel Acclamation: Everyone stands for the Gospel Acclamation and the reading of the Gospel. The Gospel Acclamation is an expression of approval and praise for that which is going to be read in the Gospel. The Alleluia is sung by the choir or cantor and then sung by all. This is usually repeated twice. If not sung, the Alleluia is omitted. During the Lenten season one of these acclamations are used in the place of the Alleluia:

- **"Praise to you, Lord Jesus Christ, King of endless glory!"**
- **"Glory and praise to you, Lord Jesus Christ!"**
- **"Praise and honor to you, Lord Jesus Christ!"**

Gospel Reading: The deacon or priest will say, *"The Lord be with you."* The congregation will respond, *"And with your spirit."* The deacon or priest will say, *"A reading from the Holy Gospel according to... [Matthew, Mark, Luke, or John]."* All will respond, *"Glory to you, Lord!"*

The Gospel reading is taken from one of the four Gospels written by either Matthew, Mark, Luke, or John. Though there are four different Gospels in the New Testament, they all tell the story of the Life of our Lord Jesus Christ. The deacon or priest will read the Gospel. When he is finished with the Gospel reading, he will proclaim: *"The Gospel of the Lord."* Everyone will respond, *"Praise to you Lord Jesus Christ."* And then all will sit for the homily.

Homily: The homily is always given by a deacon, priest, or bishop and usually explains the Church's teachings concerning the feast day being celebrated or Scripture readings from the Mass. When the homily is over, everyone stands for the Profession of Faith.

I have often heard fellow Catholics say that the Catholic Church does not use the Bible enough or that the Church's teaching should be centered more on Scripture. This saddens me, for it makes me wonder if they really understand the Mass. Even though they may be attending Mass regularly, it would appear that Mass has become a routine of worship with little active participation on their part. To help others get more out of Mass, I would recommend that they study the readings and Gospels before Mass. They can be found in the Missalette. All should try to meditate on and understand what these readings may have in common with each other and what God is trying to teach us, and then they can listen attentively during the homily to what the deacon or priest is teaching.

Profession of Faith: On Sundays and solemnities, everyone prays the Nicene Creed, which reaffirms what the Catholic Church teaches to be true. These beliefs were organized into a creed at the First Ecumenical Council at Nicene in AD 325 and were later added to and adopted at the Council of Constantinople in AD 381. The Apostles' Creed may be used at Masses with children. (The profession of faith is omitted on Ash Wednesday.)

> *"I believe in one God,*
> *the Father almighty, maker of heaven*
> *and earth,*
> *of all things visible and invisible.*
> *I believe in one Lord Jesus Christ,*
> *the Only Begotten Son of God,*
> *born of the Father before all ages.*
> *God from God, Light from Light, true God*
> *from true God, begotten, not made,*
> *consubstantial with the Father;*
> *through him all things were made.*
> *For us men and for our salvation he*
> *came down from heaven,*
> *and by the Holy Spirit was incarnate of*
> *the Virgin Mary, and became man.*
> *For our sake he was crucified under Pontius Pilate,*
> *he suffered death and was buried,*

and rose again on the third day in ac-
cordance with the Scriptures.
He ascended into heaven and is seated
at the right hand of the Father.
He will come again in glory to judge the
living and the dead and his kingdom
will have no end.
I believe in the Holy Spirit, the Lord, the
giver of life, who proceeds from the Fa-
ther and the Son, who with the Father
and the Son is adored and glorified, who
has spoken through the prophets.
I believe in one, holy, catholic and apos-
tolic Church.
I confess one baptism for the forgiveness
of sins and I look forward to the resur-
rection of the dead and the life of the
world to come. Amen."

**General Intercessions (Prayer of the
Faithful):** In the general intercessions, the
Church as a community of God's children prays
for the needs of the Church, communities, and
for all humanity. After each intention, the
commentator or priest will say, **"We pray to
the Lord,"** or something similar. And everyone
responds, **"Lord, hear our prayer,"** or another
similar verse. This concludes the Liturgy of the
Word, and everyone is seated.

LITURGY OF THE EUCHARIST

The Liturgy of the Eucharist is the second
major part of the Mass. Even though the Liturgy
of the Eucharist and the Liturgy of the Word are

distinct, they are so closely connected with each other that they form one single act of worship.[4]

The Liturgy of the Eucharist is two-fold. First, it fulfills the request Jesus gave at His Last Supper when He broke the bread and gave it to His disciples saying, *"This is my body which will be given up to you. Do this in memory of me"*[5] Second, it follows in the Hebrew tradition of giving a sacrifice to God. *The General Instruction of the Roman Missal* (GIRM) tells us that the Mass is at once a sacrifice of praise and thanksgiving, of reconciliation and expiation. At every Mass, we celebrate the mystery of Christ's death and resurrection for the forgiveness of sin and the fullness of salvation.

The Liturgy of the Eucharist is broken down into three steps: Preparation of the Altar and the Gifts, the Eucharistic Prayer, and the Communion Rite. Up to this point in the Mass, everything has taken place away from the altar at either the priest's chair or at the pulpit (ambo).

Preparation of the Altar and the Gifts: The altar is prepared as the gifts are collected. A song is normally sung during the collection, and then the gifts of bread and wine, which will become Christ's body and blood, along with the money or other gifts collected are brought forward. The gifts of bread and wine are placed on the altar and the other gifts are put in a suitable place. If no song is sung, the priest will say out loud, *"**Blessed are you, Lord God of all creation, for through your goodness we have re-***

---

[4] *Sacrosanctum Concilium*, Chapter II, Par. 56.
[5] Lk 22:19.

ceived the bread we offer you: fruit of the earth and work of human hands, it will become for us the bread of life." Everyone will respond, "Blessed be God forever."

The priest then prepares the Chalice by mixing a little water with the wine. This mixing of the water with the wine symbolizes both the divine and human nature of Jesus combined in the mystery of the Incarnation. The priest prays, "By the mystery of this water and wine may we come to share in the divinity of Christ, who humbled himself to share in our humanity." The priest will then say, "Blessed are you, Lord God of all creation, for through your goodness we have received the wine we offer you: fruit of the vine and work of human hands it will become our spiritual drink." Everyone will respond, "Blessed be God forever."

The priest washes his hands and prays in silence, "Wash me, O Lord, from my iniquity and cleanse me from my sin." This washing of the hands (though in early Christianity was most likely a necessity) has now become a symbol of internal cleansing or purification in preparation for the Eucharistic Prayer.

The priest will invite everyone to pray by saying, "Pray, brethren (brothers and sisters), that my sacrifice and yours may be acceptable to God, the almighty Father." Everyone stands and says, "May the Lord accept the sacrifice at your hands, for the praise and glory of his name, for our good, and the good of all his holy Church."

Prayer over the Gifts: In this prayer, the priest prays that God will accept our gifts and make them the sacrament of our salvation. He will either recite or sing the prayer over the gifts. When finished, the congregation will respond, *"Amen."* The Prayer over the Gifts changes daily.

Eucharistic Prayer: There are four regular Eucharistic Prayers and two special Eucharistic Prayers for Masses of Reconciliation. There are also three Eucharistic Prayers for Masses with Children or four recently approved Eucharistic Prayers for Various Needs and Occasions. The Eucharistic Prayer contains several parts: the Preface Dialogue; the Preface; the Holy, Holy, or *Sanctus*; the Epiclesis; the Institution Narrative; the Memorial Acclamation; the Anamnesis, Offering, and Intercessions; and the final Doxology and Great Amen.

I will be using Eucharistic Prayer II as an example.

Preface Dialogue: This reminds us that even though the priest prays the Eucharistic Prayer on our behalf, we all participate in the offering of this prayer.

> Priest: *"The Lord be with you."* All: *"And with your spirit."*
> Priest: *"Lift up your hearts."* All: *"We lift them up to the Lord."*
> Priest: *"Let us give thanks to the Lord, our God."* All: *"It is right and just."*

Preface: This is a prayer of praise and thanksgiving. The priest prays (Eucharistic

Prayer II), **"It is truly right and just, our duty and salvation, always and everywhere to give you thanks, Father most holy, through your beloved Son, Jesus Christ, your Word through whom you made all things, whom you sent as our Savior and Redeemer, incarnate by the Holy Spirit and born of the Virgin. Fulfilling your will and gaining for you a holy people, he stretched out his hands as he endured his Passion, so as to break the bonds of death and manifest the resurrection. And so, with the Angels and all the Saints we declare your glory, as with one voice we acclaim:"**

Holy, Holy (Sanctus): The Holy, Holy is a song of praise. As the angels sing out in angelic praise "Holy, Holy, Holy" so do we: **"Holy, Holy, Holy Lord, God of hosts, Heaven and earth are full of your glory."** As the crowds shouted praise to Jesus as He entered Jerusalem on the back of a donkey, we continue, **"Hosanna in the highest. Blessed is he who comes in the name of the Lord. Hosanna in the highest."**[6] In the United States everyone normally kneels after the Holy, Holy till the completion of the Great Amen. This posture may differ in different regions of the world.

Now comes the part of the Eucharistic Prayer when the consecration of the bread and wine takes place. The priest standing in for Jesus extends his hands over the bread and wine and prays. In doing so, the priest fulfills what Jesus instructed us to do at the Last Supper.

---

[6] Mt 21:9.

The Epiclesis (invocation of the Holy Spirit): The priest prays, *"You are indeed Holy, O Lord, the fount of all holiness. Make holy, therefore, these gifts, we pray, by sending down your Spirit upon them like the dewfall, so that they may become for us the Body and Blood of our Lord, Jesus Christ."*
Institution Narrative: The priest continues, *"At the time he was betrayed and entered willingly into his Passion, he took bread and, giving thanks, broke it, and gave it to his disciples, saying: Take this, all of you, and eat of it: for this is my Body which will be given up for you. In a similar way, when supper was ended, he took the chalice and, once more giving thanks, he gave it to his disciples, saying: Take this, all of you, and drink from it: for this is the chalice of my Blood, the Blood of the new and eternal covenant, which will be poured out for you and for many for the forgiveness of sins. Do this in memory of me."* While these prayers are being said, the priest holds up first the bread, which has become the body of Jesus Christ in veneration, and then the wine, which has become the blood of our Lord Jesus Christ.

Mystery of Faith: The priest will say, *"Let us proclaim the mystery of faith."* The congregation will respond in unison with one of the following acclamations:

A – *"We proclaim your death, O Lord, and profess your Resurrection until you come again."*

B – *"When we eat this bread and drink this cup, we proclaim your death, O Lord, until you come again."*

C - *"Save us, Savior of the World, for by your cross and resurrection, you have set us free."*

What is the mystery of faith? Several papers have been written on the Church's teachings on it, and I would suggest reading "Mysterium Fidei" (Mystery of Faith), an Encyclical Letter written by Pope Paul VI, dated September 3, 1965, for a detailed explanation. A simple explanation would be the Church's belief in the recognition and effect of Jesus' death, resurrection, and second coming on our redemption, combined with the Church's teaching that Jesus instituted the sacrament of the Eucharist at the Last Supper thereby allowing us to remember, celebrate, and offer Christ's perfect sacrifice at every Mass.

Anamnesis, Offering, and Intercessions: This is when the second part of the Eucharistic Prayer begins. "Anamnesis" means recalling to mind and celebrating what Christ has done for us by His death and resurrection. This perfect sacrifice is offered up to God during the offering, combined with prayers of thanks, unity, and petition. We pray for the Pope and the bishops. We pray for the deceased that they may be reunited with God. We pray for the unity of the Church and all its members.

The priest continues the Eucharistic Prayer: *"Therefore, as we celebrate the memorial of his Death and Resurrection, we offer you,*

Lord, the Bread of life and the Chalice of salvation, giving thanks that you have held us worthy to be in your presence and minister to you. Humbly we pray that, partaking of the Body and Blood of Christ, we may be gathered into one by the Holy Spirit. Remember, Lord, your Church, spread throughout the world, and bring her to the fullness of charity, together with N. our Pope and N. our Bishop and all the clergy. Remember also our brothers and sisters who have fallen asleep in the hope of the resurrection and all who have died in your mercy: welcome them into the light of your face. Have mercy on us all, we pray, that with the blessed Virgin Mary, Mother of God, with the blessed Apostles, and all the Saints who have pleased you throughout the ages, we may merit to be co-heirs to eternal life, and may praise and glorify you through your Son, Jesus Christ."

Doxology (praise to God) and Great Amen: This is the final praise given to God when we acknowledge Him for His sending of His Son and that everything we do, all honors and glories, is for the Almighty Father. The priest who offers the Eucharistic Sacrifice in the person of Christ raises the Vessels containing the body and blood of Christ. We as humans can offer no greater sacrifice. The priest will recite, *"Through him, with him, and in him, in the unity of the Holy Spirit, all glory and honor is yours, almighty Father, forever and ever."* The congregation responds, *"Amen."* The Amen may be sung more than once. This concludes the Eucharistic Prayer, and everyone stands for the Lord's Prayer.

COMMUNION RITE

Lord's Prayer: The priest extends an invitation for all to join in praying the Lord's Prayer. *"At the Savior's command and formed by divine teaching, we dare to say:"* Everyone will pray, *"Our Father, who art in heaven, hallowed be thy name; thy kingdom come; thy will be done on earth as it is in heaven. Give us this day our daily bread; and forgive us our trespasses as we forgive those who trespass against us; and lead us not into temptation, but deliver us from evil."* The priest will pray, *"Deliver us, Lord, we pray, from every evil, graciously grant peace in our days, that, by the help of your mercy, we may be always free from sin and safe from all distress, as we await the blessed hope and the coming of our Savior, Jesus Christ."* All will respond, *"For the kingdom, the power, and the glory are yours, now and forever."*

Sign of Peace: The priest will say, *"Lord Jesus Christ, who said to your Apostles, Peace I leave you, my peace I give you, look not on our sins, but on the faith of your Church, and graciously grant her peace and unity in accordance with your will. Who live and reign forever and ever."* All will respond, *"And with your spirit."* The priest or deacon will say, *"Let us offer each other a sign of peace."* Everyone will turn and offer those near them a sign of peace such as a handshake, hug, or kiss, depending on their relationship.

Breaking of the Bread: While the priest breaks the bread and prepares the communion vessels, everyone prays the Lamb of God (*Agnus Dei*): *"Lamb of God, you take away the sins of the world: have mercy on us. Lamb of God, you take away the sins of the world: have mercy on us. Lamb of God, you take away the sins of the world: grant us peace."* This may also be sung. When it is finished, everyone kneels.

Communion: The priest will say**, *"Behold the Lamb of God, behold him who takes away the sins of the world. Blessed are those called to the supper of the Lamb."* The congregation responds, *"Lord, I am not worthy that you should enter under my roof, but only say the word and my soul shall be healed."* Communion is then distributed with the communion minister saying, *"The body of Christ."* The communicant responds, *"Amen."* During Communion, everyone who has already made his or her First Communion and is free of mortal sin may proceed to the front of the altar to receive the sacrament.

Communion Song: A Communion song or chant is sung during the reception of Communion.

Period of Silence or Song of Praise: After the distribution of Communion is finished, everyone should sit for a period of silence for individual prayer or for the singing of a song of praise. The posture at this time may also be kneeling as long as the whole congregation is unified in its posture. When the Period of Silence or Song of Praise is finished, everyone will stand for the Prayer after Communion.

Prayer after Communion: The priest will say, *"Let us pray."* Then he will pray the Prayer after Communion. This prayer changes frequently. When the prayer is complete, everyone responds, *"Amen."* This concludes the Liturgy of the Eucharist.

CONCLUDING RITE

Announcements: It is at this time that any announcements, acknowledgements, eulogies, or reflections are given. The congregation may remain standing or be asked to sit, depending upon the length of the announcements.

Greeting: Everyone will stand for the greeting, which can be thought of as a farewell. The priest will say, *"The Lord be with you."* Everyone will respond, *"And with your spirit."*

Blessing: There are three options for the blessing. I will list the first option. The priest says, *"May almighty God bless you, the Father, and the Son, and the Holy Spirit."* Everyone responds, *"Amen."* This blessing brings the Mass to its conclusion.

Dismissal: The deacon or priest dismisses the congregation using one of the following,

- *"Go forth, the Mass has ended."*
- *"Go and announce the Gospel of the Lord."*
- *"Go in peace, glorifying the Lord by your life."*
- *"Go in peace."*

This reminds us that only through love and peace can we really serve the Lord. Everyone responds, *"Thanks be to God."*

The priest will again show reverence to the altar by kissing it as he did at the beginning of Mass. This ritual is the same as one kisses a loved one when saying goodbye, the altar being a symbol of Christ. Though it is not prescribed in the order of the Mass, a final recessional psalm or hymn may be sung as the priest and ministers leave the sanctuary. All members of the congregation are expected to remain in the sanctuary until the priest and ministers exit, out of respect, and this also allows the priest and deacon to greet everyone as they leave.

In summary, this layman's explanation of the Mass should help you understand how and why the Mass becomes the perfect offering to God. In the Introductory Rite, we prepare ourselves by prayer to celebrate the Mass. We call to mind our sins, asking God to have mercy on us. We praise and glorify God by praying the *Gloria*. In the Liturgy of the Word, we listen to what God has given to us in both the Old and the New Testament, and we receive instruction by the priest in the homily. During the Liturgy of the Eucharist, we obey the command Jesus gave us at the Last Supper. We call to mind what God did for us in sending His Son to suffer, die, and rise again so that our sins may be forgiven. During the consecration, the priest acting in Jesus' place commemorates His actions at the Last Supper. By virtue of the Sacrament of Holy Orders, the priest consecrates the bread and wine, transforming them into the body and blood of Jesus, which are then offered up to God. This perfect offering is given to us in Communion as our spiritual food. What better spiritual sacrifice can we offer?

Chapter 9

OUR BLESSED MOTHER

In my short prayer, which I mentioned earlier, I pray, "Blessed Mother, ever virgin, please pray for me." People who are not Catholic have asked why I ask the Blessed Mother to pray for me rather than pray directly to Jesus. They also ask why I say "ever virgin." To understand the answer to both of these questions, we must fully understand who Jesus is. Christians believe that Jesus is the God-Man. He is the Word made flesh. *"And the Word was made flesh and dwelt among us (and we saw his glory, the glory as it were of the only begotten of the Father), full of grace and truth. John beareth witness of him and crieth out, saying: This was he of whom I spoke: He that shall come after me is preferred before me: because he was before me. And of his fullness we all have received: and grace for grace. For the law was given by Moses: grace and truth came by Jesus Christ. No man hath seen God at any time: the only begotten Son who is in the bosom of the Father, he hath declared him"* (Jn 1:14-18). God the Son came down Himself into the flesh to suffer death and to be resurrected so that man could be freed from the clutches of death, brought upon him when he disobeyed God's commandment and ate from the Tree of Knowledge.

We know as truth that God is all good. Since Jesus was God incarnate, Jesus therefore has to be all good. Even though Jesus was human, He was still God, and being God and all good, He could not have been born with the sin of Adam, called original sin. If this was not the case and Jesus was born with the sin of Adam upon His soul, as other humans are born, He would not have been all good and therefore could not have been God. In order for Jesus to be born without this stain of sin upon His soul, His mother Mary also could not have inherited the sin of Adam. If she did, Jesus would have inherited this sin from His mother as all men do. For Mary to be the Mother of God, she had to be sinless. Scripture tells us that when the angel Gabriel appeared to Mary (Luke 1:28), his first word was *chaire*: "Hail." Hail is not a greeting that was directed at someone below your status but was used as a salutation to someone above your status as in "Hail, Caesar." This is very significant because Gabriel's greeting shows his deference to Mary, knowing that she would be the Mother of God. Gabriel's next words were *kecharitomene*: "Full of Grace." This indicates that Mary was sinless because grace and sin cannot coexist. If you are full of grace, you can have no sin. His next words were "*The Lord is with Thee.*" This visit from the angel Gabriel confirms that Mary was indeed set apart from all other women.

"Blessed" means consecrated, sacred, and holy. We are told in Scripture that Mary is blessed by God when Mary goes to visit her cousin Elizabeth. "*And it came to pass that when Elizabeth heard the salutation of Mary, the infant leaped in her womb. And Elizabeth was filled with the Holy Ghost. And she cried out with a loud voice and said: Blessed art thou among women and blessed is the fruit of thy womb*" (Lk 1:41-42). Then in Mary's Canticle she says, "*My soul doth magnify the Lord. And my spirit hath rejoiced in God my Saviour. Because he hath regarded the humility of his handmaid: for behold from henceforth all generations shall call me blessed*" (Lk 1:46-48). This verse demonstrates why we call her the Blessed Mother. For Mary to be all good she had to have been conceived without the sin of Adam (original sin) so that she would be without blemish to bear the Christ child. This is what the church calls the Immaculate (sinless) Conception. The document *Ineffabilis Deus*, an apostolic constitution issued by Pope Pius IX on December 8, 1854 states, "*at the first instance of her conception, by a singular privilege and grace granted by God, in view of the merits of Jesus Christ, the Saviour of the human race, was preserved exempt from all stain of original sin."*

Many Catholics misunderstand the Immaculate Conception, thinking it was when Jesus was conceived in Mary's womb without sexual intercourse or that Mary was conceived by the Holy Spirit. Both these understandings are incorrect. The Immaculate Conception means that Mary was conceived in the normal way by her parents, but through God's intervention, she was created without the stain of Adam's sin.

After her Son, Jesus, Mary is the holiest person to have ever walked this earth, surpassing Adam and Eve. The Blessed Mother is the new Eve, the mother of our Church. This theme is repeated in several writings of the early Fathers of the Church.

Consider the faith that the Blessed Mother had when the angel visited her: *"And Mary said to the angel: How shall this be done, because I know not man? And the angel answering, said to her: The Holy Ghost shall come upon thee and the power of the most High shall overshadow thee. And therefore also the Holy which shall be born of thee shall be called the Son of God"* (Lk 1: 34-35). It took great courage and faith to agree to this virgin birth in a time when it was justifiable to stone to death women who became pregnant out of wedlock. Scripture tells us that Mary was betrothed to Joseph, not married to him.[1]

---

[1] Mt 1:18, Lk 1:27.

What greater love could Mary have had for God than to raise His Son? Think of the emotional strength and courage it took Mary to stand at the Place of the Skull (Golgotha) and watch her Son's crucifixion and death, not fully understanding that His resurrection was coming. What suffering this must have been! What greater faith can there be than that?

When Jesus performed the first of His signs (miracles), Mary was there as a mediator between the people and Jesus. *"And the wine failing, the mother of Jesus saith to him: They have no wine. And Jesus saith to her: Woman what is that to me and to thee? My hour is not yet come. His mother saith to the waiters: Whatsoever he shall say to you, do ye"* (Jn 2:3-5). Jesus listened to His mother and provided more wine by changing the water into wine.

During Jesus' final moments before death, He said to Mary standing at the foot of the cross, *"Woman, behold thy son. After that, he saith to the disciple: Behold thy mother. And from that hour, the disciple took her to his own"* (Jn 19:26-27). This is one of the reasons why Mary is seen as the mother of all Christians.

Knowing that the Blessed Mother had such great faith and is full of grace as Scripture tells us, how can someone not understand how close she must have been to her Son, Jesus our Lord? Think how pleasing her purity and holiness is to God and what power this would give her petitions. If, as Scripture says (Jas 5:16), the prayer of a holy person is very powerful, how much must this be true of the Mother of God! People will say, "That may be so, but I still don't need

Mary to pray for me." I would counter that their understanding is wrong, and here are a few examples to explain why. If we pray daily to the Blessed Mother, asking her to intercede for us now and especially at our hour of death, she will. This is a big benefit that we will lose if we do not pray for her intercession. At the moment of death, when we pass from this world to the next, we lose our ability to pray for ourselves. This is the most critical time for our souls, for it is at this moment that we are first judged according to the way we lived our lives. We go instantly from a life of being able to obtain grace and forgiveness through acts of prayer, penance, charity, and reception of the sacraments, to a time of judgment and then retribution for our sins. How many people do we have in our lives who we are sure we can count on to pray for our souls at this critical moment? What happens if our deaths take place in an accident or if we die in our sleep or worse when no one is around? If we have honored the Blessed Mother during our lifetimes and have prayed to her, asking for her intercession at our deaths, we are guaranteed that she will do so. What better person could we have interceding for us at our deaths than Jesus' mother?

How can we be sure of this? If we study the history of the different appearances of the Blessed Mother at Lourdes, Fatima, Guadalupe, and elsewhere, we can read about the supernatural miracles that she has performed through her Son. In Lourdes, there have been over four thousand documented miracles to attest to her intercessions. There can be no doubt of the results that can be achieved by praying to our Blessed Mother.

Our goal as Christians is to become as God-like as possible. To put it another way, we are to live our lives allowing Jesus to work through us to the point where we are united with Christ on earth. What better example do we have of some-one living his or her life as God wanted than Mary?

I return now to the original question con-cerning why I say "ever virgin" in my short pray-er. The early Christians and Church Fathers attested to the fact that Mary remained forever virgin, and neither Tradition nor Scripture say that Mary gave birth to other children. The his-torical document called *Protoevangelium of James*, written around AD 120, supports the teaching of Mary's perpetual virginity. This doc-ument was written when memories of Mary's life were still vivid in the minds of many. According to the world-renowned patristic scholar Johan-nes Quasten, "The principal aim of the whole writing [*Protoevangelium of James]* is to prove the perpetual and inviolate virginity of Mary be-fore, during, and after the birth of Christ" (*Pa-trology*, 1:120–1). [2]

St. Athanasius, one of the great Fathers and Doctors of the Holy Church, writes in his *Dis-courses Against the Arians*, "*Let those, therefore, who deny that the Son is by nature from the Fa-ther and proper to his essence deny also that he*

---

[2] "Mary: Ever Virgin," *Catholic Answers*, (San Diego: Catholic Answers 2004), http://www.catholic.com/tracts/mary-ever-virgin

took true human flesh from the ever-virgin Mary."[3] Didymas the Blind of Alexandria writes, "*It helps us to understand the terms `first-born' and `only-begotten' when the Evangelist tells that Mary remained a virgin `until she brought forth her first- born son' [Matt. 1:25]; for neither did Mary, who is to be honored and praised above all others, marry anyone else, nor did she ever become the Mother of anyone else, but even after childbirth she remained always and forever an immaculate virgin.*"[4] St. Augustine teaches us, "*It was not the visible sun, but its invisible Creator who consecrated this day for us, when the Virgin Mother, fertile of womb and integral in her virginity, brought him forth, made visible for us, by whom, when he was invisible, she too was created. A Virgin conceiving, a Virgin bearing, a Virgin pregnant, a Virgin bringing forth, a Virgin perpetual. Why do you wonder at this, O man?*"[5]

St. Cyril of Alexandria, one of the Greek Fathers and Doctors of the Church, professes Mary's perpetual virginity when he proclaims, "*The Word himself, coming into the Blessed Virgin herself, assumed for himself his own temple from the substance of the Virgin and came forth from her a man in all that could be externally discerned, while interiorly he was true God. Therefore he kept his Mother a virgin even after her childbearing.*"[6]

---

[3] St. Athanasius, *Discourses Against the Arians*, Vol. 2,70.

[4] Didymas, "The Trinity," 3:4.

[5] St. Augustine, *Sermons*, 186:1.

[6] St. Cyril of Alexandria, *Against Those Who Do Not Wish to Confess That the Holy Virgin is the Mother of God*, 4.

Let us look at the sin of Adam (original sin). By being immaculately conceived, Mary did not suffer this stain upon her soul. Therefore, Mary's desires would not be disordered as ours can be because of the effect of original sin. Without disordered passions and desires, it would be a lot harder for the devil to stir up temptations of the body, such as sexual desire, or lust for someone or something. Since Mary did not have these desires of the flesh, why would she want to have sexual relations with Joseph? We as humans tend to think of our own sexual desires and assume that Mary would feel the same. This is a wrong assumption.[7]

There is a tradition that claims Mary took a vow of virginity, and if this tradition is true, Joseph would have known of this vow before becoming betrothed to Mary and by doing so would have indicated that he accepted her vow. Her vow of virginity even adds a stronger case as to why she would remain a virgin.

People will question, "If that is true, why does Scripture say Jesus had brothers?" I'm going to quote Father John Echert because he does a great job of explaining the use of the term "brothers" in Scripture. Father Echert has a Licentiate in Sacred Scripture (S.S.L.) degree from the Pontifical Biblical Institute in Rome. He writes,

---

[7] For a good understanding of how concupiscence remains after baptism, read St Augustine's *On Marriage and Concupisence*, Book I, AD 419, and Book II, AD 420.

"The Gospel of St. Mark—with parallels in the other Synoptics--records: 6:2-3: *"And on the sabbath he began to teach in the synagogue; and many who heard him were astonished, saying, "Where did this man get all this. What is the wisdom given to him? What mighty works are wrought by his hands! Is not this the carpenter, the son of Mary and brother of James and Joses and Judas and Simon, and are not his sisters here with us?""* With regards to the "brothers" of Jesus (and sisters), we must keep in mind the original culture and languages, both spoken and written. For the Hebrews and Semitic peoples in general, the use of the word "brother" can represent a much broader range of relationship than merely a sibling. And though written in the Greek, the NT is reflecting Aramaic and this Hebrew culture. In fact, Hebrew and Aramaic did not have a particular word for cousins and other such relatives, and so "brothers" and "sisters" was generically used for such. Hence, the Septuagint (Greek version of the OT) and the New Testament adopt this feature of the Semitic languages, which they reflect, even though Greek has a particular word for cousins. A search of the OT, whether in Hebrew or the Greek Septuagint, and the NT, reveals a number of instances in which "brother" (or sister) refers to any number of relationships: BROTHER BY NATURE (siblings) Gen 4:1-2: *"Now Adam knew Eve his wife, and she conceived and bore Cain, saying: I have gotten a man with the help of the LORD. And again, she bore his brother Abel. Now Abel was a keeper of sheep, and Cain a tiller of the ground.*"

BROTHER BY KINSHIP Gen 13:8: "*Then Abram said to Lot: Let there be no strife between you and me, and between your herdsmen and my herdsmen; for we are brothers (i.e. related, as uncle and nephew).*"

BROTHER BY RACE Gen 19:4-7: "*But before they lay down, the men of the city, the men of Sodom, both young and old, all the people to the last man, surrounded the house and they called to Lot, "Where are the men who came to you tonight? Bring them out to us, that we may know them." Lot went out of the door to the men, shut the door after him, and said, "I beg you, my brothers, do not act so wickedly.*"

BROTHER BY LOVE 2 Sam 1:26: "*I am distressed for you, my brother Jonathan; very pleasant have you been to me; your love to me was wonderful, passing the love of women*" (David of his friend Jonathan). Rom 12:10: "*Love one another with brotherly affection; outdo one another in showing respect.*" Rom 14:10: "*Why do you pass judgment on your brother? Or you, why do you despise your Brother?*" (Paul speaking of Christians).

"The commentaries and homilies of the early Church accept the perpetual virginity of Mary without question. And, as the

Church teaches, when the Fathers & Doctors of the Church are in agreement on a point of Scripture, we accept this as reflecting divine revelation as a manifestation of Tradition. Aware of such texts as Mark 6:3, the Patristics (Church Fathers) commented upon a resolution to the texts. The tendency of the Western Fathers was to suggest the range of meanings for the word "brother" as I have noted above and assumed such references were to cousins. The tendency of certain Eastern Fathers was to suggest that St. Joseph was a widower who had children by a previous marriage. Regardless, we know by the certitude of tradition that these cannot have been siblings of our Lord. And, in fact, there is evidence in the NT itself, which would suggest that they were not siblings. For one thing, two of the "brothers" mentioned in this text (James and Joseph) are later described as sons of a Mary other than the Blessed Mother, and that they were cousins. Secondly, it would be inconceivable that our Lord would give His Mother into the care of the apostle John, if he had so many brothers and sisters as siblings, who would assume such a responsibility. So both the external witnesses and the Scriptures themselves support our belief in this matter."[8]

---

[8] Father Echert S.S.L., EWTN, "Catholic Q&A," 8 July 2004.

Many Christians are unaware of the limitations that apply when trying to translate the Hebrew culture and Aramaic language into Greek. Once this is understood, it is easier for them to understand the correct interpretation of "the brother of the Lord." They are surprised when they find out that Mary's perpetual virginity was believed by the early Christians and accepted as a teaching of the Scriptures. Even the early Protestant reformers believed in Mary's perpetual virginity. Martin Luther, Huldreich Zwingli, and John Calvin all believed in the perpetual virginity of Mary. Martin Luther writes, "*Christ our Savior was the real and natural fruit of Mary's virginal womb. . . . This was without the cooperation of a man, and she remained a virgin after that.*"[9] Huldreich Zwingli, who was one of the major forces in the reformation, wrote in 1524 a sermon titled "Mary, ever virgin, mother of God" in which he states, "*I have never thought, still less taught, or declared publicly, anything concerning the subject of the ever Virgin Mary, Mother of our salvation, which could be considered dishonourable, impious, unworthy or evil...I believe with all my heart according to the word of holy gospel that this pure virgin bore for us the Son of God and that she remained, in the birth and after it, a pure and unsullied virgin, for eternity.*" John Calvin writes in defense of the perpetual virginity of the Blessed Mother,

---

[9] Martin Luther, *On the Gospel of St. John: Luther's Works*, Vol. 22, Ed. Jaroslav Pelican, (St. Louis: Concordia, 1957), 23.

There have been certain folk who have wished to suggest from this passage [Matt 1:25] that the Virgin Mary had other children than the Son of God, and that Joseph had then dwelt with her later; but what folly this is! For the gospel writer did not wish to record what happened afterwards; he simply wished to make clear Joseph's obedience and to show also that Joseph had been well and truly assured that it was God who had sent His angel to Mary. He had therefore never dwelt with her nor had he shared her company... And besides this Our Lord Jesus Christ is called the first born. This is not because there was a second or a third, but because the gospel writer is paying regard to precedence. Scripture speaks thus of naming the first-born whether or not there was any question of the second.[10]

The Blessed Mother is indeed special to our Father. Recognizing her uniqueness allows us to have another weapon in our arsenal when battling against Satan and his demons.

The fourth commandment is to honor thy father and mother. Since Mary is the mother of all Christians, we are obliged to honor her. The key word is to "honor." We honor her, but we do not worship her. We worship only God. So I pray, "Blessed Mother, ever virgin, please pray for me."

---

[10] John Calvin, "Sermon on Matthew," (1562), 1:22-25.

Chapter 10

PRAYING THE ROSARY

One of the best ways to advance in your spiritual journey is to pray the Rosary. When praying the Rosary, you come closer to God by meditating on Jesus' life, while at the same time requesting for the intercession of Our Blessed Mother.

BEGINNING:

Start by holding the crucifix between your thumb and first finger:

1. Make the **Sign of the Cross**[1] and say the **Apostles' Creed.**
2. Move to the first bead and say the **Our Father**.
3. Say three **Hail Marys,** one for each of the next three beads. These three Hail Marys are said for an increase in the theological virtues of faith, hope, and charity.
4. Say the **Glory Be**.

A DECADE OF THE ROSARY:

1. Announce the First Mystery, then say the **Our Father** on the large bead.
2. Say ten **Hail Marys**, one for each bead while meditating on the Mystery.
3. Say the **Glory Be,** and, if you wish, say the **Fatima Prayer** in the space between the last of the small beads and the large bead. This completes one decade of the Rosary.

CONCLUSION:

After completion of the fifth or twentieth decade, say the **Hail, Holy Queen.** This completes the Rosary. Different regions of the world have different customs when it comes to ending the Rosary. In the United States it is becoming customary after the Hail Holy Queen to recite a closing prayer.

---

[1] Refer to page 244 on how to make the Sign of the Cross.

The Mysteries of the Rosary are to be meditated on, one per decade. To recite the prayers without meditating on the mysteries of Christ is to miss the essence of praying the Rosary. By focusing on the mysteries as you pray the Hail Mary, the Rosary truly becomes a spiritual itinerary in which Mary acts as mother, teacher, and guide, sustaining the faithful by her powerful intercession.[2] By tradition these Mysteries are used on the following days:

> **Sunday**: *The Glorious Mysteries*
> **Monday**: *The Joyful Mysteries*
> **Tuesday**: *The Sorrowful Mysteries*
> **Wednesday**: *The Glorious Mysteries*
> **Thursday**: *The Luminous Mysteries*
> **Friday**: *The Sorrowful Mysteries*
> **Saturday**: *The Joyful Mysteries*[3]

The Joyful Mysteries:

1. The Annunciation of Gabriel to Mary (Luke 1:26-38).
2. The Visitation of Mary to Elizabeth (Luke 1:39-56).
3. The Birth of Our Lord (Luke 2:1-21).
4. The Presentation of Our Lord (Luke 2:22-38).
5. The Finding of Our Lord in the Temple (Luke 2:41-52).

---

[2] John Paul II, *Apostolic Letter*, "Rosarium Virginis Mariae," (16 October 2002), 37.

[3] Ibid, 38.

IN SEARCH OF TRUTH

The Luminous Mysteries:

1. The Baptism of Our Lord in the River Jordan (Mt 3:13-16).
2. The Wedding at Cana when Christ Manifested Himself (Jn 2:1-11).
3. The Proclamation of the Kingdom of God (Mark 1:14-15).
4. The Transfiguration of Our Lord (Mt 17:1-8).
5. The Institution of the Holy Eucharist at the Last Supper (Mt 26).

The Sorrowful Mysteries:

1. The Agony of Our Lord in the Garden (Mt 26:36-56).
2. The Scourging of Our Lord at the Pillar (Mt 27:26).
3. The Crowning of the Thorns (Mt 27:27-31).
4. The Carrying of the Cross by Our Lord (Mt 27:32).
5. The Crucifixion of Our Lord (Mt 27:33-56).

The Glorious Mysteries:

1. The Glorious Resurrection of Our Lord (Jn 20:1-29).
2. The Ascension of Our Lord into Heaven (Luke 24:36-53).
3. The Decent of the Holy Spirit at Pentecost (Acts 2:1-41).

4. The Assumption of Our Blessed Mother into Heaven.
5. The Coronation of Mary as Queen of Heaven and Earth.

The Sign of the Cross:

In the name of the Father, and of the Son, and of the Holy Spirit. Amen.

The Apostles' Creed:

I believe in God, the Father, Almighty, Creator of heaven and earth; and in Jesus Christ, His only Son, our Lord; who was conceived by the Holy Spirit, born of the Virgin Mary, suffered under Pontius Pilate, was crucified; died, and was buried. He descended into hell; the third day He arose again from the dead; He ascended into heaven, sits at the right hand of God the Father Almighty; from there He shall come to judge the living and the dead. I believe in the Holy Spirit, the Holy Catholic Church, the communion of Saints, the forgiveness of sins, the resurrection of the body, and life everlasting. Amen.

The Our Father:

Our Father, who art in heaven, hallowed be Thy name: Thy kingdom come: Thy will be done on earth as it is in heaven. Give us this day our daily bread: and forgive us our trespasses as we forgive those who trespass against us. And lead us not into temptation: but deliver us from evil. Amen.

The Hail Mary:

Hail Mary, full of grace; the Lord is with thee: blessed art thou among women, and blessed is the fruit of thy womb, Jesus. Holy Mary, Mother of God, pray for us sinners, now and at the hour of our death. Amen.

Glory Be to the Father:

Glory be to the Father, and to the Son, and to the Holy Spirit; as it was in the beginning, is now, and ever shall be, world without end. Amen.

The Fatima Prayer:

O my Jesus, forgive us our sins. Save us from the fires of Hell; lead all souls into Heaven, especially those in most need of Thy mercy. Amen.

The Hail, Holy Queen:

Hail, Holy Queen, Mother of Mercy, our life, our sweetness, and our hope. To thee do we cry, poor banished children of Eve; to thee do we send up our sighs, mourning and weeping in this valley, of tears. Turn, then, most gracious Advocate, thine eyes of mercy toward us; and after this our exile show unto us the blessed fruit of thy womb, Jesus; O clement, O loving, O sweet Virgin Mary.

When the Rosary is being prayed in a group setting this is added:

V. *Pray for us, O holy Mother of God.*
R. That we may be made worthy of the promises of Christ.

Let us pray:

O God, whose only begotten Son, by His life, death, and resurrection has purchased for us the rewards of eternal life, grant, we beseech Thee, that meditating upon these mysteries in the most Holy Rosary of the Blessed Virgin Mary, we may imitate what they contain, and obtain what they promise: through the same Christ our Lord. Amen.

Most Sacred Heart of Jesus, have mercy on us.
Immaculate Heart of Mary, pray for us.

"As sailors are guided by a star to the port, so are Christians guided to Heaven by Mary." -- St. Thomas Aquinas (AD 1225-1274)

Chapter 11

THE LOST TREASURES

In my research into and study of the early Fathers of the Church and Saints, I have discovered that two keys to improving our spirituality have been mostly disregarded in today's Christianity. They are the practice of "fasting" and "doing penance." Why these important treasures have been disregarded, in my opinion, can be attributed to the lack of understanding the harmful effects sin has on us and on society as a whole and to the secularization of the Christian religion.

We're told in Scripture that fasting and do-ing penance are very important to our spiritual lives, yet very little is taught about them in to-day's religious training outside of seminaries. To prove my point, ask your Christian friends when the last time was they fasted or did penance outside the sacrament of Penance?

Fasting was a common practice in the Old Testament. Moses tells us in Deuteronomy 9:9-10, "*When I went up into the mount to receive the tables of stone, the tables of the covenant which the Lord made with you. And I continued in the mount forty days and nights, neither eating bread, nor drinking water.*" Daniel tells us, "*And I set my face to the Lord my God, to pray and make supplication with fasting and sackcloth and ashes*" (Dn 9:3). The second book of Samuel tells us how David fasted for seven days for his son.[1] The practice of fasting is mentioned again in Esther where we read, "*And again Esther sent to Mardochai in these words: Go, and gather to-gether all the Jews whom thou shalt find in Susa, and pray ye for me. Neither eat nor drink for three days and three nights: and I with my handmaids will fast in like manner, and then I will go in to the king, against the law, not being called, and expose myself to death and to dan-ger*" (Esth 4:15-16).

We know that Jesus fasted for forty days when He went out into the desert where He was tempted by the devil.[2] Does Jesus want us to fast? Consider Jesus' "Sermon on the Mount"

---

[1] 2 Sam 12:16-20.
[2] Mt 4:2.

and read His words: *"But thou, when thou fast-est anoint thy head, and wash thy face"* (Mt 6:17). He does not say "if you fast." He says "when you fast." This implies that He expects us all to do some type of fasting.

After Jesus' death and resurrection, did His followers fast in the early Church? Scripture tells us "yes." We read in Acts 13:1-3, *"Now, there were in the church which was at Antioch prophets and doctors, among whom was Barna-bas and Simon who was called Niger, and Lucius of Cyrene and Manahen who was the foster brother of Herod the tetrarch, and Saul. And as they were ministering to the Lord and fasting, the Holy Ghost said to them: Separate me Saul and Barnabas, for the work whereunto I have taken them. Then they, fasting and praying and impos-ing their hands upon them, sent them away."*

In Acts 14, Luke the Evangelist tells us, *"And when they had ordained to them priests in every church and had prayed with fasting, they commended them to the Lord, in whom they be-lieved."* (Acts 14:2). Paul speaks of fasting in 2 Corinthians 6:4-5 when he writes, *"But in all things let us exhibit ourselves as the ministers of God, in much patience, in tribulation, in necessi-ties, in distresses, in stripes, in prisons, in sedi-tions, in labors, in watchings, in fastings."* Paul mentions fasting again in chapter 11 when he explains about the hardships that he has en-countered: *"In labor and painfulness, in much watchings, in hunger and thirst, in fastings often, in cold and nakedness"* (2 Cor 11:27).

> *"Fasting begets prophets and strengthens strong men. Fasting makes lawgivers wise; it is the soul's safeguard, the body's trusted comrade, the armor of the champion, the training of the athlete." -- St. Basil, Bishop of Caesarea (AD 330-379).*

We also learn from early Church writings that fasting was a part of a Christian's life. The *Didache* (The Teaching of the Twelve Apostles), which was written in AD 70 states, *"But before the baptism let the baptizer fast, and the baptized, and whoever else can; but you shall order the baptized to fast one or two days before.* In the following chapter it states: *But let not your fasts be with the hypocrites, for they fast on the second and fifth day of the week. Rather, fast on the fourth day and the Preparation (Friday)."*[3]

St. Polycarp in his letters to the Philippians, writes, *"let us return to the word which has been handed down to us from the beginning; 'watching unto prayer,' and persevering in fasting; beseeching in our supplications the all-seeing God 'not to lead us into temptation,' as the Lord has said: 'The spirit truly is willing, but the flesh is weak'."*[4]

Why is fasting important? It is important because it is good for both our bodies and for our souls. In fasting, the body cleanses itself of

---

[3] *Didache*, 7:1; 8-1.

[4] St. Polycarp, *Epistle of Polycarp to the Philippians*, Roberts-Donaldson translation, 7.

its bodily waste and toxic impurities. Paul teaches us that the body is a temple of the Holy Spirit.[5] We are expected to take care of our bodies, and proper fasting can be used to improve our health. Fasting should not be used to diet and lose weight.

There are several reasons why fasting is good for our spiritual lives. It makes us recognize our reliance on God. It allows us to express our commitment to Him. It gives us a way to share in Jesus' suffering. It helps to liberate us from our wants and desires. The great saints teach us that this liberation from our physical desires is so important in advancing in our spiritual lives. Fasting also helps us build humility, as we read in Ezia (Esdras) 8:21-23, *"And I proclaimed there a fast by the river Ahava that we might afflict (humble) ourselves before the Lord our God, and might ask of him a right way for us, and for our children, and for all our substance. ... And we fasted, and besought our God for this: and it fell out prosperously unto us."*

We know that fasting, when combined with prayer and faith is a powerful weapon against sin and spiritual warfare. When Jesus was returning from Mount Tabor with Peter, James, and John, the nine other apostles were busy trying to cast out a demon from a boy. The demon had made the boy mute and would throw the boy down on the ground and cause him to foam at the mouth and grind his teeth. The nine apostles were having no success at driving the demon out of the boy. Jesus returning from the

---

[5] 1 Cor 6:19.

mount saw that a large crowd had gathered. Upon seeing Jesus, they ran up and asked for His help. Jesus asked the boy's father a few questions and then commanded the spirit to leave the boy and never return. [6] Later, in private the apostles ask Jesus, *"Why could not we cast him out? Jesus said to them: Because of your unbelief. For, amen I say to you, if you have faith as a grain of mustard seed, you shall say to this mountain, Remove from hence hither, and it shall remove; and nothing shall be impossible to you. But this kind is not cast out but by prayer and fasting"* (Mt 17:18-20).

Father Gabriele Amorth, the chief Exorcist of Rome who has performed hundreds of exorcisms, confirms that fasting is a powerful weapon against demons when he states in his book, *"Jesus says that to cast out a particular kind of demon three things are required: faith, prayer, and fasting. These are still the most efficacious methods."*[7]

When you fast, it should be a joyful fast. Jesus instructs us in Matthew 6:16-18, *"And when you fast, be not as the hypocrites, sad. For they disfigure their faces, that they may appear unto men to fast. Amen I say to you, they have received their reward. But thou, when thou fastest anoint thy head, and wash thy face: That thou appear not to men to fast, but to thy Father who is in secret: and thy Father who seeth in secret will repay thee."*

---

[6] Mk 9:14-18.

[7] Gabriele Amorth, *An Exorcist: More Stories*, (San Francisco: Ignatius, 2002), 191.

Let us look at the Catholic Church's laws on abstinence and fasting.

Abstinence: All who have reached their fourteenth birthday are to abstain from eating meat on Ash Wednesday and on all Fridays during Lent.[8] A lot of Catholics, since Vatican II, have a misunderstanding about Fridays being a day of abstinence and penance. Canon Law 1250 states, *"The days and times of penance for the universal Church are each Friday of the whole year and the season of Lent."* I recommend you reread that statement. Then Canon Law 1251 states, *"Abstinence from meat, or from some other food as determined by the Episcopal Conference, is to be observed on all Fridays, unless a solemnity should fall on a Friday."*[9] The U.S. Bishops issued a letter on November 18, 1966, called "The Pastoral Statement on Penance and Abstinence." In this statement they proclaim, *"We hereby terminate the traditional law of abstinence as binding under pain of sin, as the sole prescribed means of observing Friday, we give first place to abstinence from flesh meat. We do so in the hope that the Catholic community will ordinarily continue to abstain from meat by free choice as formerly we did in obedience to Church law."* The bishops did not take the act of doing penance out of Fridays. By taking the sin out of abstaining from meat on Fridays, they were allowing Catholics to freely make, *"every Friday a day of self-denial and mortification in prayerful remembrance of the passion of Jesus*

---

[8] *Canon Law*, 1252.
[9] See chapter 15 for a list of solemnities.

Christ." The problem lies in the fact that most Catholics have taken up the practice of eating meat on Fridays while ignoring the importance of making Friday a day of self-denial, mortification, and prayer.

Fasting: All those who are eighteen and older, until their fifty-ninth birthday, are instructed to fast on Ash Wednesday and Good Friday.[10] Only one full meal is allowed on days of fast. Two other meals, sufficient to maintain strength, may be taken according to our needs. But together, they should not equal a full meal. Liquids are allowed between meals. The obligation to fast on these two days does not apply to those with serious health problems. We are required to fast (abstain) from any food and drink for one hour before the reception of the Eucharist, except for water and medicine.[11]

One can see that the obligation to fast is a very minimum requirement, and we should strive to use these guidelines as a starting point from which to grow. The first thing you want to consider when starting to fast is your health. If you are pregnant, do not fast. If you have any known medical conditions or are taking any medications, be sure to check with your physician before starting. It is best both physically and spiritually to start slowly.

The fast that I like to do is called a twenty-four-hour fast. It is relatively easy to accomplish, yet hard enough that we will gain spiritually from it when the fast is done with prayer

---

[10] Canon Law, 1251-1252.
[11] Ibid., 919.

and proper intentions. Since the American Bishops in their 1966 Pastoral Statement told us to make "every Friday a day of self-denial," this fast will work well in fulfilling their direction and at the same time in commemorating the suffering of our Lord when He died on the cross.

The fast will last from dinner (supper) Thursday night till dinner Friday night. Eat a normal dinner on Thursday night. Be sure not to snack before going to bed. This part is easy to do, and by the time you wake in the morning, you will have completed half your fast. When you first get up in the morning, after saying your prayers, drink two glasses of water. This will help your stomach from feeling empty. I like to do the same at lunchtime. Instead of eating lunch, take the time to pray. I personally like to say a Rosary.

You will find the hardest time of the fast to be in the early afternoon when your habitual eating habits tell you that you need to eat. Ignore these cravings and offer them up to God. If you absolutely feel that you must have something, you can drink a little fruit juice. This will help to satisfy your cravings. Remember that man can go weeks without eating food, and a few more hours will not physically hurt you. Keep busy, and before you know it, it will be dinnertime, and you will have completed your fast. The key is to keep your mind busy. Remember, fasting should always be combined with prayer, especially at the beginning and the end of the fast.

Doing the twenty-four-hour fast this way allows us to complete the fast in private as Jesus taught us to do.[12] You can even do your fast when you are out of town on business or have a dinner engagement to attend. If your business meeting requires a lunch instead of dinner, just start your fast earlier to correspond with the time of your luncheon.

You can begin by doing the twenty-four-hour fast on the first Friday of the month. Then as you progress, set a goal of doing it every Friday. What better way to help prepare for the celebration of the Eucharist than to join in our Lord's suffering by doing penance and fasting on Fridays to commemorate His Passion?

Once you have grown accustomed to fasting, you may want to try a forty-hour fast in remembrance of Jesus' forty days and nights of fasting in the desert.[13] This can be done for special occasions, such as a death of a close friend, a special feast day in the Church, or Holy Week. I would recommend doing your forty-hour fast as a bread and water fast. You are allowed to have plain bread, with no butter or spreads, along with water. Do not use bread that contains nuts, fruits, or other fillers. It is best to use home-cooked bread rather than the supermarket bread, which contains little nutrition. This will help make it easier for you to complete your fast. You can eat as much bread as you feel you need to complete your fast, but remember you are fasting, and strive to eat as little as possible. Again, it is very important that you combine your fast with prayer. After you have completed

---

[12] Mt 6:16-18.
[13] Mt 4:2.

several forty-hour fasts, you may want to extend them to a three-day fast. I would not recommend fasting longer than three days without proper guidance from a spiritual director and your physician.

Fasting helps us identify with the poor and hungry of this world. St. Augustine's writings teach us that we should fast for the poor. When we fast, we should take the money that we would have spent for our food and use it to help feed the poor. By doing this, we fulfill all three forms of penance that Jesus' gave instruction on: fasting, prayer, and almsgiving.[14]

The second treasure that Christianity has slowly begun to disregard is the practice of penance. What is penance? Penance is a combination of having disdain and grief for our sins because of our love for God, along with the intention to reform our lives and a willingness to perform satisfaction for our sins.

The Church teaches us that taking up our cross each day and following Jesus is the surest way of penance.[15] If you read the writings by the great saints, you will discover that they understood this teaching well. To state it simply, doing penance is showing your love for God. If you do something that harms a loved one, once you realize what you have done, don't you try to make up for it? A man has a fight with his wife and says things in anger that he doesn't really mean. What does he do? He first tells her he's sorry. He then takes her out to dinner, buys her

---

[14] Mt 6:1-18.
[15] CCC, 1435; Lk 9:23.

flowers, or helps around the house. He does this to make up for his actions. It is the same when you love God. You try to make up for your wrong-doings through penance.

There are many different types of penance we can do. I will list a few.

Help the poor. This can be done in numerous ways such as donating our time and money to charities that specialize in feeding and clothing the poor or going on mission trips. These are excellent ways to expiate (atone for) our sins.

Visit the elderly, lonely, and the imprisoned, especially during the holidays when they feel the loneliest.

Fast. This does not have to be limited to food. We can fast from our favorite drinks such as soda, coffee, or beer. We can abstain from things that we love to do, such as watching television, going to the movies, eating out, or playing sports such as golf, fishing or bowling.

Pray and meditate for a specific amount of time each day. We can pray devotions such as the Rosary, or we can choose a set number of our favorite prayers to pray each day. We can rise earlier than normal to pray, thus sacrificing sleep.

Read spiritual works, such as Scripture or writings of the saints. I would caution you against reading the New Age writers. I would start with the New Testament. Once I have read it in its entirety, I would read the Old Testament. Upon its completion, I would start reading the writings of the Doctors of the Church. See chapter 13 for reference.

Refrain from talking for a set amount of time. St. Teresa tells us in *The Way of Perfection* that silence and solitude are a great help in prayer.[16] **Help your neighbor** or one who you know is in need.

These are just a few examples of penances we can perform. All the penances listed above have one thing in common. They are all signs of love. Work at making penance a part of your life, and it will transform your heart.

---

[16] Teresa of Avila, *The Way of Perfection* (New York: Doubleday, 1991), 56.

"Slander is a poison which kills charity, both in the slanderer and the one who listens." -- St Bernard (AD 1090-1153)

Chapter 12

JUDGING OUR GROWTH

Developing the habit of daily prayer is one of the first steps in building our relationship with God. Taking time to pray when we first wake up in the morning and again before we fall asleep at night helps to bring God to the forefront of our lives. Add prayers and meditation during the day and you will find yourself building a good spiritual foundation. But is this enough to live God's will? Let's listen to what Jesus teaches us in Matthew 7:21: "*Not every one that saith to me, Lord, Lord, shall enter into the kingdom of heaven: but he that doth the will of my Father who is in heaven."* It is not enough just to pray to God. We must transform our lives by following the will of God. We accomplish this by living the Gospels.

Jesus teaches us that the second greatest commandment is to love our neighbor as ourselves.[1] That we must "love our neighbors as ourselves" is mentioned seven times in the New Testament and once in the Old Testament.[2] When Jesus uses the term "neighbor," He does not mean only the person who lives next door, our close friends, or our countrymen. He means all God's children, and this includes our enemies.

We are told, *"He that hath the substance of this world and shall see his brother in need and shall shut up his bowels from him: how doth the charity of God abide in him? My little children, let us not love in word nor in tongue, but in deed, and in truth "*(1 Jn 3:17-18). John is telling us that our love for God is shown through our charitable deeds and that it is not in what we say but in what we do that we manifest God's love.

We must learn to be charitable to all men and especially help those who are less fortunate. We can do this by feeding the hungry and clothing the naked; by visiting the sick and lonely, especially the elderly; and by refraining from slander and gossip.

---

[1] Mk 12:31.
[2] Mt 19:19, Mt 22:39, Mk 12:31, Lk 10:27, Rm 13:9, Gal 5:14; Jm 2:8, Lvt 19:18.

We can volunteer our time, talents, and wealth. On the spiritual plane, we can perform charitable acts through prayer and fasting.

How can we be sure that we're staying on the right track in living the Gospels? To do so, we must form a habit of judging our daily actions against how God wants us to live our lives. This is called examining our conscience. As a professional athlete studies films of his past performances to find and correct his mistakes, so must we review and examine our actions throughout the day. This allows us to see what we could have done better and what sins we have committed and need to confess.

Confession of sins goes back to the early Church. Jesus says, *"Whether is easier, to say, Thy sins are forgiven thee: or to say, Arise, and walk? But that you may know that the Son of man hath power on earth to forgive sins, (then said he to the man sick of palsy,): Arise, take up thy bed and go into thy house. And he arose and went into his house. And the multitude seeing it, feared, and glorified God that gave such power to men"* (Mt 9:5-7). This authority to forgive man's sins was passed down to the apostles and the early Church by Jesus after His resurrection. Scripture tells us, *"The disciples therefore were glad, when they saw the Lord. He said therefore to them again: Peace be to you. As the Father hath sent me, I also send you. When he had said this, he breathed on them; and he said to them: Receive ye the Holy Ghost. Whose sins you shall forgive, they are forgiven them: and whose sins you shall retain, they are retained"* (Jn 20:20-23). This is not to say that man forgives sins.

Only God can forgive sins. Jesus is giving the apostles and His Church the authority to exercise this power in God's name.

We know and understand that this forgiving of sins that Jesus commissioned his apostles to do is meant for their successors in the Church. We read in Matthew 16:18-19 that Jesus tells Peter, *"And I say to thee: That thou art Peter; and upon this rock I will build my church. And the gates of hell shall not prevail against it. And I will give to thee the keys of the kingdom of heaven. And whatsoever thou shalt bind upon earth, it shall be bound also in heaven: and whatsoever thou shalt loose upon earth, it shall be loosed also in heaven.*

Why is confession of our sins in the sacrament of Penance (Reconciliation) so important in building a strong relationship with God? Why can't we just ask God for forgiveness instead of going through another human being? There are several reasons why it is good to go to a priest to confess one's sins. First, we are doing what Scripture asks us to do. In James 5:16, James tells us, *"Confess therefore your sins one to another: and pray one for another, that you may be saved."* He then continues to teach, *"For the continual prayer of a just man availeth much."*[3] In the sacrament of Penance, the priest prays for us. He has dedicated his life to God and intercedes and prays on our behalf, and his prayer, as Scripture tells us, is very powerful.

---

[3] In some translations of the Bible, the "just" man is translated as a "holy man" or "religious" man.

It is important for us to remember that in the sacrament of Penance one is confessing his sins to God and asking God's forgiveness, not the priest's. The priest is there as God's representative to give the penitent counseling and advice, to assign him a penance and tell him what type of reparations he must do if required, and then grant him absolution, which means pardon and peace for our sins.

Confession is good for both our bodies and souls. Guilt can cause both emotional and physical illness to the body. Knowing that the priest has taken a vow of secrecy known as the "Seal of Confession," which prevents him from talking about or revealing our sins, frees us to talk openly about our sins, such as: physically or verbally abusing our spouses or children, acting on homosexuality, committing adultery, viewing pornography, gambling excessively, becoming drunk, engaging in lurid sexual behavior, and abusing drugs. By confessing these types of sins, we can release the guilt that we carry because of our actions. At the same time, being able to discuss why we do such acts and receiving instruction on how to change these actions and bad habits, while resolving never to repeat them, is helping ourselves both physically and emotionally. Where else can we go to receive this type of help for free?

The second and most important part of confession is what it does to our relationship with God. It restores us spiritually back into the grace of God and at the same time reconciles us with the Church.[4] The Catholic Church teaches that the sacrament of Penance has six spiritual effects:

- Reconciliation with God by which the penitent recovers grace;
- Reconciliation with the Church;
- Remission of the eternal punishment incurred by mortal sins;
- Remission, at least in part, of temporal punishments resulting from sin;
- Peace and serenity of conscience, and spiritual consolation;
- An increase of spiritual strength for the Christian battle.[5]

What great spiritual gifts these are! I believe there is no greater relief than when we leave confession after hearing the priest, acting on God's behalf, grant us absolution for our sins.

Another reason why regular confession is good for building a strong relationship with God is that it forces us to examine our conscience on a regular basis. Regularly examining our conscience helps us to discover how sinful we really are and how we must strive at all times to obey God's will. Becoming aware of temptation and being able to recognize it at its first appearance is one of the best steps in combating sin. It is so easy to see other people's sins, but recognizing and admitting to ourselves our own sins is much harder. We are all sinners, and due to our

---

[4] CCC, 1469.
[5] Ibid., 1496.

weakened nature, it is impossible not to sin, but the degree to which we sin can be greatly reduced by becoming aware of our weaknesses and inclination towards various types of sins. For instance, if we have an inclination to gossip when we are with certain individuals, being able to recognize this weakness will allow us to consciously avoid the situation in which we are inclined to gossip.

Confession is not a "get out of jail free" card. We cannot expect to be forgiven without any intention of our changing our sinful ways. The Church teaches us, *"The sacrament of Penance is a whole consisting in three actions of the penitent and the priest's absolution. The penitent's acts are repentance, confession or disclosure of sins to the priest, and the intention to make reparation and do works of reparation."*[6] This means that when we go to confession, we first must feel contrition for our sins. What exactly is contrition? Contrition is "sorrow of the soul and detestation for the sin committed, together with the resolution not to sin again."[7] Then we must confess our sins to a priest who will give us a penance for our sins. This penance is to help correct the harm and make satisfaction for the sins we have committed. For instance, if we have stolen from someone, we normally are told to return the stolen goods. If we have told a lie that has slandered someone, we may be told to restore that person's reputation by admitting our lie. We may be told to say a certain number of

---

[6] Ibid., 1491.
[7] *Council of Trent* (1551): DS, 1676.

prayers or to perform charitable works. This penance generally corresponds to the gravity of our sins. When the priest is finished imposing our penance, he will ask us to recite our act of contrition, which is a prayer in which we tell God that we are sorry for our sins and resolve to sin no more.[8]

Examining our conscience is comparing our daily actions against the Ten Commandments and natural law. Listed below is a sample.

Examination of Conscience

I. "I am the Lord, thy God, thou shall not have strange gods before Me."

   1. Have I sinned against Christ by seriously believing in New Age religion, Scientology, astrology, horoscopes, fortune-telling, superstition, or the occult?
   2. Have I endangered my Catholic faith or caused scandal by associating with anti-Catholic groups and associations (e.g., the Freemasons)?
   3. Has fame, fortune, money, career, pleasure, or anything else replaced God as my highest priority?
   4. Have I neglected my daily prayers?

II. "Thou shall not take the name of the Lord thy God in vain."

---

[8] The Act of Contrition can be found in Section B, Prayers.

1. Have I committed blasphemy by using the name of God and Jesus Christ to swear rather than to praise?
2. Have I committed sacrilege by showing disrespect to holy objects (e.g., crucifix, Rosary) or contempt for religious persons (e.g., bishop, priests, deacons, religious women) or for sacred places (e.g., a Church)?
3. Have I committed sacrilege by going to Holy Communion in the state of mortal sin without first going to confession, i.e., after missing Mass on Sunday or a Holy day?
4. Did I violate the one-hour fast before Communion?
5. Did I break the laws of fast and abstinence during Lent?
6. Did I neglect my Easter duty to receive Holy Communion?
7. Have I neglected to support the Church and the poor by sharing my time, talent, and treasure?

III. "Remember to keep holy the Lord's (Sabbath) day."

1. Did I miss Mass on *any* Sunday or Holy Day of Obligation? (Bad weather and sickness are acceptable reasons.)
2. Have I shown disrespect by leaving Mass early, not paying attention, or not joining in the prayers?

3. On Sunday, did I do unnecessary work, which could have been done the day before?
4. Have I been stingy in my support for the Church?
5. Do I give of my time and talent?

IV. "Honor thy Father and Mother."

Parents:

1. Have I set a bad example for my children by casually missing Mass, neglecting prayer, or ignoring my responsibility to provide a Catholic education by either sending my children to parochial school or to C.C.D. (a religious education program)?[9]
2. Do I show little or no interest in my children's faith and practice of it?
3. Have I showed disrespect for those in authority, government, or Church?
4. Have I not expressed my moral values to them?

Children:

1. Have I been disobedient and/or disrespectful to my parents or guardians?
2. Did I neglect to help them with household chores?

---

[9] Confraternity of Christian Doctrine.

3.   Have I caused them unnecessary worry and anxiety by my attitude, behavior, or moods?

V. "Thou shall not murder."

1. Did I consent, recommend, advise, approve, support, or have an abortion?
2. Did I realize that there is an excommunication for anyone who procures an abortion?
3. Did I actively or passively cooperate with an act of euthanasia, whereby ordinary life support means were stopped, or means were taken to directly end the life of an elderly or sick person?
4. Have I committed an act of violence or abuse (i.e., physical, sexual, emotional or verbal)?
5. Have I endangered the lives of others by reckless driving or by driving under the influence of drugs or alcohol?
6. Do I show contempt for my body by neglecting to take care of my own health?
7. Have I been mean or unjust to anyone?
8. Have I held a grudge or sought revenge against someone who has wronged me?
9. Do I point out others' faults and mistakes while ignoring my own?

10. Do I complain more than I compliment?

11. Am I ungrateful for what other people do for me?

12. Do I tear people down rather than encourage them?

13. Am I prejudiced against people because of their color, language, or ethnic-religious background?

VI. "Thou shall not commit adultery."

1. Have I been faithful to my marriage vows?

2. Have I encouraged others to remarry outside the Church?

3. Have I committed fornication or adultery?

4. Did I have any sex before or outside of marriage?

5. Did I commit the sins of masturbation and/or artificial contraception?

6. Do I view pornographic material (i.e., via magazines, videos, internet, or hotlines)?

7. Have I gone to massage parlors or adult bookstores?

8. Have I not avoided the occasions of sin (persons or places), which would tempt me to be unfaithful to my spouse or to my own chastity?

9. Do I encourage and entertain impure thoughts and desires?

10. Do I tell or listen to dirty jokes?

VII. "Thou shall not steal."

1. Have I stolen, vandalized, or damaged the property of others?
2. Have I cheated at school?
3. Am I faithful to my promises?
4. Do I give an honest day's work to my employer?
5. Have I been honest in paying my taxes, and prompt in paying my debts?
6. Have I stolen any object, committed any shoplifting, or cheated anyone of his or her money?
7. Did I knowingly deceive someone in business or commit fraud?
8. Have I shown disrespect or even contempt for other people's property?
9. Have I done any acts of vandalism?

VIII. "Thou shall not bear false witness against thy neighbor."

1. Have I told a lie or spread rumors, which may ruin someone's reputation (sin of calumny, or slander)?
2. Have I told a lie in order to deceive someone?
3. Have I told the truth with the purpose and intention of ruining someone's reputation (sin of detraction)?
4. Did I commit perjury by falsely swearing an oath on the Bible?
5. Am I a busybody, or do I love to spread gossip and secrets about others?

6. Do I love to hear bad news about my enemies?

IX. "Thou shall not covet thy neighbor's wife."

1. Have I looked lustfully at persons of the opposite sex?
2. Have I said or done anything to disrespect or weaken another person's marriage?

X. "Thou shall not covet thy neighbor's goods."

1. Am I greedy or envious of another's goods?
2. Do I let financial and material concern, or the desire for comfort, override my duty to God, to Church, to my family, or to my own spiritual well being? [10]

Developing the habit of examining your conscience on a regular basis will enable you to better judge how you are living the Gospels. It will make you more aware of your faults, which will enable you to have a better chance to correct them. By going to confession on a regular basis, you are doing what Scripture tells us to do, and at the same time you are receiving the graces of the sacrament, which strengthens us in our battle against sin.

---

[10] Adapted from "Sacrament of Penance: Examination of Conscience," courtesy of Father John Trigilio, Jr., Ph.D.

Chapter 13

THE JOURNEY

You will not find God unless you go looking for Him. God loves all His children and wants us to come to Him, but He will not force us to love Him. This is a decision that one must make personally. It is not one that can be made by our parents, friends, or spouse. Only you can make this important decision.

Once you make the decision spiritually to journey towards God, your life will change. There will be little changes, at first hardly noticeable, but as you progress in prayer, your knowledge and wisdom will grow. You will discover God everywhere. You'll find Him in the sweet smell of springtime, the freshly plowed earth. You'll see God in the beauty of a bud as it blossoms into a flower. Go for a walk in the woods, and God will be there with you. He'll be in the rustling of the trees. You'll feel his breath as a warm breeze blows across your face. You'll see God in the little squirrels and bunnies as they romp through the brush. Go into the city, and He'll be there. You'll hear Him in a baby's crying. You'll see Him in the beauty of a woman or the handsomeness of a man, and yes, you'll see Him in the poverty of a street person. If you take the time to search and open your mind, you'll find that God is everywhere.

In searching for God, you will also find the effects of Satan and his legion of demons. Today in our society, people no longer want to believe in the evil one. It is much easier to convince ourselves that he does not exist and therefore has no power over us. Very seldom in this modern era will you hear a sermon in a Catholic church about the temptations of the devil. It is not in vogue, and therefore, many priests hesitate to preach the truth of the evil one for fear of upsetting their congregations. The easier path is to preach that God is all-loving, but this in itself misleads some into an illusion that everyone dies and goes to Heaven. I wish it were so, but that is not the message that Jesus and His disciples taught. It is not what the Church and Scripture and the great Doctors of the Church teach. Do not make this mistake. It is much easier to fight an adversary that you recognize exists than one that you choose to ignore, because he will not ignore you. Satan appears in Scripture numerous times under numerous names. To list a few: the Serpent (Gen 3:1-2, 4, 13-14); Beelzebub (Mt 10:25); the father of lies (Jn 8:44); the Dragon (Rev 12); and the evil one (Mt 5:37); and in Revelations 9:11, he is called angel of the bottomless pit, Apolloyn, Abaddon, and Exterminans.

People will ask, "How do we know Satan exists if we can't see him?" As with God, if you look for him you will find him. You can see Satan in the addictions of sex, drugs, and alcohol. You'll hear him in the fights, beatings, and killings in the streets and on the news. He's in the sexual assaults and the kidnappings. You'll find him behind the power-hungry personnel of local churches and ecclesiastical communities. He's behind the making of pornography, and in the rage and selfishness of mankind!

Do not be alarmed, for even though Satan is a great threat to our spiritual salvation, he is powerless against our Almighty Father. Ask God, His angels, and His saints to protect you, and you will be guarded. This is not to say that you will not be tempted, for even our Lord was tempted.[1] The closer you get to God, the greater the threat you become to Satan and the more he will try to derail you and draw you from your spiritual path. But do not fear, for the closer the union you form with God, the better you are prepared to fight off Satan's temptations.

---

[1] Mt 4:1.

When you take a journey through unfamiliar territory, the smart thing to do is find a guide familiar with the area to show you the way. Where can you find this guide? In the Gospel of John, Jesus says, *"I am the way, and the truth, and the life. No man cometh to the Father, but by me."*[2] Jesus died to release the bands that were holding mankind in bondage, allowing us to rejoin the Father. Jesus knew that He would be leaving us after His resurrection to return to his Father, so He established His Church and sent us the Holy Spirit to help guide us on our journey to union with the Father. God has given us Scripture, along with saintly men and women through the generations to help us understand more fully His teachings.

It is difficult to make a spiritual journey by yourself. There are so many distractions along the way that can throw you off the correct path. When you read the writings of the great saints, you'll discover that most of them had spiritual directors to help guide them on their journey. Today in our country, it is hard to find a qualified spiritual director. With the shortage of priests, many are overworked and lack the time. Many are not knowledgeable enough in the contemplative life to be of much assistance. Because of these difficulties, it may take you years to find a qualified director. In the meantime, great guidance can be found in the writings of the Doctors of the Church.

If you are looking for spiritual guidance in your journey towards achieving union with our

---

[2] Jn 14:6.

Father, the books listed below will be helpful. There are many great writings, and this is just a small sample of them.

- *The Confessions* by Saint Augustine, translated by Maria Boulding, O.S.B., Vintage Books. ISBN 0-375-70021-8.
- *The Life of Teresa of Jesus: The Autobiography of Teresa of Avila*, translated by E. Allison Peers, Image Books, Doubleday. ISBN 0-385-01109-1.
- *The Collected Works Of Saint John of The Cross*,[3] translated by Kieran Kavanaugh, O.C.D., and Otilio Rodriguez, O.C.D., ICS Publications. ISBN 0-935216-14-6.
- *Saint Therese of Lisieux: The Story of the Soul*, translated by John Beevers, Image Books, Doubleday. ISBN 0-385-02903-9.
- *Fire Within: St. Teresa of Avila, St. John of the Cross, and the Gospel-on Prayer* by Thomas Dubay, S.M., Ignatius Press. ISBN 0-89870-263-1.
- *The Way of Perfection: Teresa of Avila*, translated by E. Allison Peers, Image Books, Doubleday. ISBN 0-385-065-39-6.
- *Seeking Spiritual Direction: How to Grow the Divine Life Within* by Thomas Dubay, S.M., St. Anthony Messenger Press. ISBN 0-89283-810-8.

---

[3] This is one of the most spiritually rewarding and insightful books that I have ever read.

- *Introduction to the Devout Life* by Saint Francis de Sales, Vintage Spiritual Classics. ISBN 978-0-375-72562-3.
- *Diary: Divine Mercy in My Soul* by Saint Maria Faustina Kowalska, Marian Press. ISBN 978-1-59614-189-6
- *Early Christian Writings: The Apostolic Fathers*, translated by Maxwell Staniforth, revised by Andrew Louth, Penguin Books. ISBN0 14-044475-0.

Life is full of choices. It is not only the big choices but also the little choices that we make daily that decide that path on which we travel through life. When you first wake up in the morning, greet God and thank Him for the new day. Take time throughout the day to talk to Him. Take even more time to listen.

> *"For by listening to man, we gain knowledge of human realities, but by listening to God we gain knowledge of divine things known as wisdom."*
> *- - St. Thomas Aquinas* [4]

When times are good, take the time to thank God. When times are bad, offer your pain and sufferings as penance for your sins and the sins of mankind. When you perform your job, do it to the best of your ability in honor of God. When you see other people sinning, look at your own sins and ask forgiveness and strive to do better. When being tempted, fight back. Say a prayer to

---

[4] Thomas Aquinas, *Summa Theologica*, la, Q1:6 RD.

St. Michael to help fight off the temptation. Strive to forgive people who have done you harm, and pray for understanding.

In my personal journey, I have come to understand that God is my reason for being. Not only is God for me, but I am for Him. I'm here to love Him and praise Him. I look to God as my friend, my helper, my counselor, my protector, and most of all, my lover. When I say "lover," I do not mean that in a sensual but in an emotional way. Remember the first time you fell in love. The great feeling it gave you. You couldn't stop thinking about the other person. They were always on your mind. You always wanted to please them. You wanted to share everything with them. That is the feeling you want to strive for in your relationship with God.

"Be still and see that I am God"[1]

---

[1] Psalm 45[46]:11

Chapter 14

COMMON QUESTIONS

In this chapter, I'm going to cover questions that I have throughout the years wondered about, or have heard other people ask. They will be listed in no special order. I hope that you will find the simple explanations to these questions helpful in your journey toward union with God.

What did Jesus mean when He said, "Blessed are the poor in spirit; for theirs is the kingdom of God?" (Mt 5:3). The common thought many have when first hearing this verse is how can the poor in the Holy Spirit enter the kingdom of God. Their confusion comes from the misunderstanding of inserting the Holy Spirit for spirit. When the Holy Spirit was called the Holy Ghost no one would think of the word "spirit" as being part of the Blessed Trinity. If you look at the definition of "spirit" as being a will, outlook, or disposition of mind, this verse becomes easy to understand. "Poor in spirit" means living your life as a poor man or to live your life without being focused on riches. Jesus tells us: *"Amen, I say to you that a rich man shall hardly enter into the kingdom of heaven"* (Mt 19:23). The reason why it is hard for a rich man to enter heaven is because his riches easily become idols and distractions from daily prayer and honoring and praising God. This self-centered pursuit of material things makes it much harder for someone to become detached from his wealth and material possessions, which all the great saints tell us is a requirement to achieve union with God. Also, money in our society is many times associated with honor, and the pursuit of self-honor is damaging to our souls, for we know that all gifts on this earth come from God.

> *"The soul that is attached to anything however much good there may be in it, will not arrive at the liberty of divine union. For whether it be a strong wire rope or a slender and delicate thread that holds the bird, it matters not, if it really holds it fast; for, until the cord be broken the bird cannot fly." -- St. John of the Cross (AD 1542-1591)*

Is the Sabbath really Saturday, or is it Sunday? Let's begin by finding when the first mention of the Sabbath appears in Scripture. It first appears in Exodus when Moses instructs the Israelites after they collect the manna. *"But on the sixth day they gathered twice as much, that is, two gomors every man: and all the rulers of the multitude came, and told Moses. And he said to them: This is what the Lord hath spoken: Tomorrow is the rest of the sabbath sanctified to the Lord"* (Ex 16:22-23).

The next mention of the Sabbath is when the Lord delivers the Ten Commandants to Moses and Aaron. *"Remember that thou keep holy the sabbath day. Six days shalt thou labour, and shalt do all thy works. But on the seventh day is the sabbath of the Lord thy God: thou shalt do no work on it, thou nor thy son, nor thy daughter, nor thy manservant, nor thy maidservant, nor thy beast, nor the stranger that is within thy gates. For in six days the Lord made heaven and earth, and the sea and all things that are in them, and rested on the seventh day: therefore the Lord blessed the seventh day, and sanctified it"* (Ex 20:8-10). By this Scripture, we know that the Sabbath was the seventh day of the week, which was Saturday. It started at sunset Friday night and ended at sunset Saturday night.

People will ask: "If the Sabbath is Saturday, then why did the Christians change their worship to Sunday?" First, the Church did not change the Sabbath from Saturday to Sunday. The Sabbath was part of the Old Mosaic Covenant, which God made with the Hebrews. The Sabbath is still Saturday, but Christians worship on Sunday, the Lord's Day, which is the first day of the week. We know that Jesus honored the Sabbath but He felt the laws concerning the Sabbath had become so restrictive that He even questioned them, stating, *"The sabbath was made for man, not man for the sabbath"* (Mk 2:27). When Jesus healed a woman who had been crippled by a spirit for eighteen years, He was attacked by the leader of the synagogue for curing on the Sabbath.[1]

It was on Sunday, the first day of the week, that Jesus' resurrection was discovered when Mary of Magdala came to the tomb early in the morning and saw that the stone had been removed. It was also on Sunday that Jesus first appeared to His disciples. *"Now when it was late that same day, the first of the week, and the doors were shut, where the disciples were gathered together, for fear of the Jews, Jesus came and stood in the midst, and said to them: Peace be to you"* (Jn 20:19). God also chose Sunday to have the Holy Spirit descend down upon the apostles, which is known in the Church as Pentecost Sunday. These are some of the reasons why Sunday is known as the Lord's Day.

Historians do not know exactly when the Christians started meeting to worship and receive the Eucharist on the Lord's Day, but Tradition and Scripture teach us that Jesus Himself initiated it. We read in Luke that two of the apostles on the road to Emmaus meet Jesus, and towards evening He breaks the bread with them: *And it came to pass, whilst he was at ta-*

---

[1] Lk 13:10-16.

ble with them, he took bread and blessed and brake and gave to them" (Lk 24:30).

We also know Paul's Letter to the Romans, written around AD 57-58, states, *"For one judgeth between day and day: and another judgeth every day. Let every man abound in his own sense. He that regardeth the day regardeth it unto the Lord"* (Rom 14:5-6). This is one of the first statements in Scripture about worshiping on Sunday, versus the Sabbath. Later, while in prison, Paul wrote his letters to the Colossians, stating, *"Let no man therefore judge you in meat or in drink or in respect of a festival day or of the new moon or of the Sabbaths, Which are a shadow of things to come: but the body is of Christ"* (Col 2:16-17). This would indicate that there was already discussion amongst the Gentiles and Christian Jews about the worshipping on the Lord's Day versus the Sabbath. Luke tells us in the book of Acts: *"And on the first day of the week, when we were assembled to break bread, Paul discoursed with them, being to depart on the morrow: And he continued his speech until midnight"* (Acts 20:7). By this passage we know that the apostles were meeting on the Lord's Day rather than the Sabbath to worship and receive the Eucharist.

We know as the differences between the new Christian sect (under the New Covenant) and the Jewish sect (under the Old Mosaic Covenant) grew, worshiping on the Lord's Day rather than the Sabbath helped distinguish and separate the two sects. In Syria, following the death of St. John, the last apostle, a guide for the teaching of Christians was written, called the

"Teaching of the Twelve Apostles," or the *Dida-che*. The *Didache* teaches, *"On the Lord's own day, gather together and break bread."* This is a clear reference, written around AD 100, invoking Christians to worship on Sunday.[11]

In AD 110, only twelve years after the death of St. John, Ignatius, Bishop of Antioch, calls the Sabbath "antiquated." The full passage of the letter of St. Ignatius to the Magnesians reads, *"Do not be led astray by other doctrines nor by old fables which are worthless. For if we have been living by now according to Judaism, we must confess that we have not received grace. The prophets . . . who walked in ancient customs came to a new hope, no longer Sabbatizing but living by the Lord's day, on which we came to life through Him and through His death."*[12]

The change from worshiping on the Sabbath to the Lord's Day was started by the apostles shortly after the Resurrection of the Lord. It seems to have happened for two main reasons: First, Jewish Christians initially wanted to avoid separating from the Jewish religion, but as the Gentiles were baptized into the sect and the New Covenant was preached, this led to a total distinction and separation of the two sects. Second, Sunday appeared to be special to God, for He chose it for Jesus' resurrection and appearing to the apostles after His resurrection and for the descending of the Holy Spirit on Pentecost. So the early Church chose Sunday to worship and

---

[11] James P. Guzck, "From Sabbath to Sunday," (San Diego: This Rock, February 1999).
[12] Ibid.

celebrate the breaking of the bread (Mass), to honor the Lord on His day.

Why does the deacon or priest along with the congregation cross themselves on their forehead, lips, and hearts before the reading of the Gospel, and what does this symbolize? They begin with the signing of the cross on the forehead to indicate that to be a good Christian, we must first use our minds to seek out and discover God's existence. God added the choice of free will to our intellect so that we can choose for ourselves how we want to live our lives. It is up to us as individuals to decide if we are going to spend our life living in our faith and having our love of God at the forefront of our daily thoughts and actions. By crossing our forehead, we are indicating that our faith and knowledge of God is in our minds. We then cross our lips because to be a good Christian, we must not only think of God but must strive to live the words of God with our own words, speaking of and praising Him daily. By crossing the heart, we indicate that if we have God continually on our minds and in our words, we cannot help but have Him in our hearts.

If one is baptized as a Protestant and then becomes a Catholic, must one be baptized again? Baptism is the door or entryway into the Christian journey. Jesus teaches us that without being baptized, we cannot enter the kingdom of Heaven.[2] In Baptism, through the grace of the Holy Spirit, we receive a bath that

---

[2] Jn 3:5.

purifies, justifies, and sanctifies.[3] We are not baptized into each individual denomination but baptized into the Christian life. In order for the Church to recognize the sacrament of Baptism, it must be done with the same intention that the Church has and in the correct matter and form. The matter in Baptism is the water and the form would be the Trinitarian formula that we are taught in Matthew 28:19: *"Going therefore, teach ye all nations; baptizing them in the name of the Father, and of the Son, and of the Holy Ghost."* Once we have been baptized with water in the name of the Father, and of the Son, and of the Holy Spirit, there would be no reason to be re-baptized since we have already been validly baptized and have received God's graces of Baptism.

Why does the Church use incense during some of her ceremonies? Scripture tells us that incense is pleasing to God. In the Old Covenant, God instructs Moses to burn a mixture of incense as an offering because it is considered sacred to God.[4] In the book of Revelation, an angel uses incense as an offering to God.[5] The Church thinks of the sweet-smelling smoke of incense as a symbol of our prayers rising to Heaven and purifying whatever it touches. The priest may use incense during Mass to bless the altar during the introductory rites. He may also use it during the offertory to bless the bread and wine, the crucifix, the altar, the congregation, and himself. Incense may be used in proces-

---

[3] CCC, 1227.
[4] Ex 30:34-37.
[5] Rev 8:3-4.

sions and when blessing items, and in the Benediction of the Blessed Sacrament. It is also used on Holy Saturday when the priest inserts five grains of incense into the paschal candle during its blessing. The five grains symbolize the five wounds of Christ. They are usually enclosed in pieces of wax resembling nails and are inserted into the wax of the candle in the form of a cross.

Why does the Church sign people's foreheads with ashes on Ash Wednesday? Lent is a time for spiritual renewal of our faith. It is a time for prayer, fasting, penance, and contrition for our sins. Ash Wednesday is the first day of the Lenten fast. It is officially known as the "Day of Ashes," and even though it is not a holy day of obligation, it is one of the Church's most popular days. It is a day of fast and abstinence.

Ash Wednesday occurs forty-six days before Easter and forty days before Good Friday, not counting Sundays. Sunday is left out of Lent because it is the Lord's Day; it is a day of celebration, instead of penance. The ashes are prepared by the burning of the blessed palms from Palm Sunday of the previous year. The ashes are blessed. Four prayers are said over them and then they are sprinkled with Holy water and incensed.[6] The deacon or priest usually signs the ashes unto our foreheads in the shape of a cross while reciting one of two formulas. The first and most common formula is, "Remember man that thou art dust and unto dust thou shalt return."

---

[6]New Advent, "Ash Wednesday," *Catholic Encyclopedia*, http://www.newadvent.org/cathen/01775b.htm.

This comes from Genesis 3:19 and reminds us of our mortality. We recognize that our life span, compared to the history of man, is indeed a very short time, and as man before us has come and gone, so will we. Therefore, we must make use of our time wisely while we still can to repent and do penance for our sins. The second formula consists of the words, "Turn away from sin and be faithful to the Gospel." This reminds us of our baptismal vows to reject sin and to live the Gospels.

The signing of the cross on the forehead with ashes is also a sign of ownership. It professes that we belong to Jesus Christ, who gave His life on the cross for us. We do not wash the ashes off our foreheads but wear them throughout the day till they naturally wear off. This is not done for the reason of pride, which Scripture warns us against in Matthew, but as a symbol of our love for Christ and as a remembrance and thanksgiving for His Passion.

Chapter 15

KNOWLEDGE OF THE FAITH

E very Catholic should invest time in becoming
knowledgeable in his or her faith. The greater
understanding we have of spiritual matters, the
better chance we have of living God's will. Famil-
iarizing ourselves with the items listed below will
help all Christians to better understand the
Catholic faith.

The Four Pillars of the Catholic Faith:

- Faith –The Apostles' Creed
- The Seven Sacraments

IN SEARCH OF TRUTH

- The Ten Commandments
- Prayer –The Lord's Prayer

The Ten Commandments:

1. Thou shall not have other gods before (besides) Me.
2. Thou shall not take the Name of the Lord thy God in vain.
3. Remember to keep holy the Lord's (Sabbath) day.
4. Honor thy father and thy mother.
5. Thou shall not murder (kill).
6. Thou shall not commit adultery.
7. Thou shall not steal.
8. Thou shall not bear false witness against thy neighbor.
9. Thou shall not covet thy neighbor's wife.
10. Thou shall not covet thy neighbor's goods.

The Seven Sacraments:

- Baptism
- Confirmation (known as "Chrismation" in the Eastern churches)
- Penance (Conversion, Confession, Reconciliation)
- Eucharist
- Matrimony
- Holy Orders
- The Anointing of the Sick (Extreme Unction)

The Precepts of the Church: Precepts are laws made by the Church. They are set to govern the **minimum** amount of prayer and penance to help us grow spiritually in love of God and our neighbors.[1]

1. You shall attend Mass on Sundays and holy days of obligation and rest from servile labor.
2. You shall confess your sins at least once a year.
3. You shall receive the sacrament of the Eucharist at least during the Easter season.
4. You shall observe the days of fasting and abstinence established by the Church.
5. You shall help to provide for the needs of the Church.

The Seven Capital (deadly) Sins: These are called "capital sins" because all sins stem from one of these seven. Listed to their right are their opposing capital virtues.

• Pride	Humility
• Greed	Liberality
• Lust	Chastity
• Anger	Meekness
• Gluttony	Temperance
• Envy	Brotherly love
• Sloth	Diligence

---

[1] CCC, 2041-2043.

The Seven Gifts of the Holy Spirit (Sanctifying): The origin of these gifts is taken from Isaiah 11:1-3.

- Wisdom
- Understanding
- Counsel
- Fortitude
- Knowledge
- Piety
- Fear of the Lord[2]

The Four Cardinal Virtues: Cardinal virtues can be obtained through human effort.

- Prudence
- Justice
- Temperance
- Fortitude

The Theological Virtues: The theological virtues are supernatural in nature and cannot be obtained by human effort.

- Faith
- Hope
- Charity (love)[3]

The Twelve Fruits of the Holy Spirit:

- Charity

---

[2] CCC, 1831.

[3] A supernatural virtue that helps us love God above all things and to love others for God's sake.

- Longanimity (long suffering)
- Joy
- Mildness
- Peace
- Faith
- Patience
- Modesty
- Benignity
- Continence (self-control)
- Goodness
- Chastity

Works of Mercy: Works of Mercy are charitable acts by which we come to the aid of our neighbor in his spiritual and bodily necessities. There are seven works called the Corporal Works of Mercy, which aid in bodily necessities, and there are seven works called the Spiritual Works of Mercy, which aid in spiritual necessities.[4]

Corporal Works of Mercy:

- Feed the hungry.
- Give drink to the thirsty,
- Clothe the naked.
- Shelter the homeless.
- Visit the sick.
- Visit the imprisoned.
- Bury the dead.

---

[4] CCC, 2447.

IN SEARCH OF TRUTH

Spiritual Works of Mercy:

- Admonish the sinner.
- Instruct the ignorant.
- Counsel the doubtful.
- Comfort the sorrowful.
- Bear wrongs patiently.
- Forgive all injuries.
- Pray for the living and the dead.

Holy Days of Obligation in the United States:

- Immaculate Conception- December 8
- Christmas-December 25
- Mary, Mother of God-January 1
- The Ascension-Thursday of the sixth week of Easter (unless transferred to the following Sunday)
- The Assumption of the Blessed Mother- August 15
- All Saints Day- November 1

Solemnity: A day of celebration in the Church's liturgical calendar. Solemnities celebrate important events in the life of Jesus, Mary, and the Saints, beginning on the evening before the actual date. "Solemnity" comes from the Latin words *solet* and *annus* – meaning a yearly celebration.[5]

- Mary, Mother of God
  January 1

---

[5] New Advent, "Solemnity," *Catholic Encyclopedia*, http://www.newadvent.org/cathen/14133a.htm.

- Epiphany Sunday between January 2 and January 8
- Joseph, Husband of Mary
March 19
- Annunciation
March 25
- Easter Triduum Date varies between March and April
- Ascension of the Lord
40 days after Easter
- Pentecost
50 days after Easter
- Holy Trinity
Sunday after Pentecost
- Body and Blood of Christ
Sunday after Holy Trinity
- Sacred Heart Friday after Body and Blood of Christ
- Birth of John the Baptist
June 24
- Peter and Paul, Apostles
June 29
- Assumption of the Blessed Mother
August 15
- All Saints
November 1
- Christ the King November, the last Sunday of ordinary time
- Immaculate Conception
December 8
- Christmas
December 25

The Stations of the Cross: There are fourteen Stations of the Cross, which are usually represented by pictures or plaques hung on the walls of a Catholic church. Each one represents an event in the final hour of our Lord's life, starting with the condemnation by Pontius Pilate and ending with the burial of our Lord's body in the tomb. (The Resurrection of Christ is often used as a Fifteenth Station.) The Stations of the Cross are traditionally prayed during the Fridays of Lent.

1. Jesus is condemned to death.
2. Jesus is made to carry His cross.
3. Jesus falls the first time.
4. Jesus meets His Blessed Mother.
5. Simon of Cyrene helps Jesus carry His cross.
6. Veronica wipes Jesus' face.
7. Jesus falls the second time.
8. Jesus meets the women of Jerusalem.
9. Jesus falls the third time.
10. Jesus is stripped of His garments.
11. Jesus is nailed to the cross.
12. Jesus dies on the cross.
13. Jesus is taken down from the cross.
14. Jesus is laid in the tomb.

The Eight Beatitudes: Jesus begins his first sermon in the book of Matthew with these eight blessings.[6]

- Blessed are the poor in spirit: for theirs is the Kingdom of Heaven.

---

[6] Mt 5:3-10.

- Blessed are the meek: for they shall possess the land.
- Blessed are they who mourn: for they shall be comforted.
- Blessed are they that hunger and thirst after justice: for they shall have their fill.
- Blessed are the merciful: for they shall obtain mercy.
- Blessed are the clean of heart: for they shall see God.
- Blessed are the peacemakers: for they shall be called children of God.
- Blessed are they that suffer persecution for justice' sake, for theirs is the Kingdom of Heaven.

PART TWO

Prayers and Meditations

SECTION A

DOCTORS OF THE CHURCH

The title "Doctor of the Church" is a special honor given to certain canonized saints in recognition of their outstanding contributions made to the understanding and development of Christian doctrine. The word "doctor" means "teacher." To become a Doctor of the Church one must meet three conditions: eminent learning, a high degree of sanctity, and proclamation by the Church.[1] Eminent learning means he or she has

---

[1] New Advent, "Doctors of the Church," *Catholic Encyclopedia*, http://www.newadvent.org/cathen/05075a.htm.

a depth of understanding or insight into the teachings of Christ and the Traditions of the Catholic faith. This doctrinal insight must have been written down and explained in writings or homilies that the Church feels have great value to its members. To become a Doctor, one must have lived a life of sanctity considered outstanding, even when compared to other saints. This special honor is issued by the Congregation of Sacred Rites and bestowed by the Pope after a careful examination of the saint's writings.[2]

There are thirty-three Doctors of the Church. The first eight listed are called "Ecumenical Fathers" because of their widespread influence. The first four listed came from the Western (Latin-speaking) half of the Roman Empire. The next four listed came from the Eastern (Greek-speaking) Roman Empire. Reading and studying the writings from the Church Doctors can be helpful in your spiritual journey. Their writings can be used as a focal point for prayer and meditation.

St. Ambrose, Father of the Church, AD 340-397.
St. Jerome, Father of the Church, AD 345-420.
St. Augustine, Father of the Church, AD 354-430.
St. Gregory the Great (Pope), Father of the Fathers, AD 540-604.
St. Athanasius, Father of the Church, AD 295-373.

---

[2] This does not imply that their writings are totally free from error.

St. Basil the Great, Father of the Church, AD 330-379.

St. Gregory of Nazianzus, Father of the Church, AD 330-390.

St. John Chrysostom, Father of the Church, AD 345-407.

St. Ephraem the Deacon, Father of the Church (Syriac), AD 306-373.

St. Hilary, Father of the Church (Latin), AD 315-368.

St. Cyril of Jerusalem, Father of the Church (Greek), AD 315-387.

St. Cyril of Alexandria, Father of the Church (Greek), AD 376-444.

St. Leo the Great (Pope), Father of the Church (Latin), AD 390-461.

St. Peter Chrysologus, Father of the Church (Latin), AD 400-450.

St. Isidore of Seville, Father of the Church (last Latin), AD 560-636.

St. John Damascene, Father of the Church (last Greek), AD 676-749.

St. Bede the Venerable, AD 673-735.

St. Peter Damian, AD 1007-1072.

St. Anselm, AD 1033-1109.

St. Bernard of Clairvaux, AD 1090-1153.

St. Anthony of Padua, AD 1195-1231.

St. Albert the Great, AD 1200-1280.

St. Bonaventure, AD 1217-1274.

St. Thomas Aquinas, AD 1225-1274.

St. Catherine of Siena, AD 1347-1379.

St. Teresa of Avila, AD 1515-1582.

St. Peter Canisius, AD 1521-1597.

St. John of the Cross, AD 1542-1591.

St. Robert Bellarmine, AD 1542-1621.

St. Lawrence of Brindisi, AD 1559-1619.
St. Francis de Sales, AD 1567-1622.
St. Alphonsus Liguori, AD 1696-1787.
St. Therese of Lisieux, AD 1873-1897.

SECTION B

PRAYERS

This section is designed to bring you closer to God through prayer. By devoting five to ten minutes of prayer: in the morning, at three o'clock, and at night, you will start to develop a closer relationship with God. Pray the prayers in the order that they are listed. If you pray them humbly, you will discover a change taking place in your heart and soul.

When you first start, if you are time limited, you can pray the Three O'clock Prayers every Friday.

Then as your prayer life expands, add them to your daily prayers except for on the Lord's Day.

As you progress in prayer, add the Rosary, the Devine Mercy Chaplet, the Efficacious Novena to the Sacred Heart of Jesus, etc. You should also include reading a few verses from the gospels and then meditate on what you have just read. This quiet time will allow God to speak to you.

WHY WE MUST PRAY

"In whatever state the soul may be, it ought to pray. A soul which is pure and beautiful must pray, or else it will lose its beauty; a soul which is striving after this purity must pray, or else it will never attain it; a soul which is newly converted must pray, or else it will fall again; a sinful soul, plunged in sins, must pray so that it might rise again. There is no soul which is not bound to pray, for every single grace comes to the soul through prayer....Let the soul be aware that, in order to pray and persevere in prayer, one must arm oneself with patience and cope bravely with exterior and interior difficulties. The interior difficulties are discouragement, dryness, heaviness of spirit and temptations. The exterior difficulties are human respect and time; one must observe the time set apart for prayer." "Divine Mercy in My Soul" by Saint Faustina.

MORNING PRAYERS

Start with the **Sign of the Cross**.

Lord Jesus Christ, Son of God, have mercy on me a sinner.

I praise Thee, O Lord; I adore Thee, O Lord; I bless Thee, O Lord; Glory be to God on high; O Lord, I sing thy glory.

GLORIA

Glory to God in the highest, and on earth peace to people of good will. We praise You, we bless You, we adore You, we glorify You, we give You thanks for Your great glory, Lord God, heavenly King, O God, almighty Father. Lord Jesus Christ, Only Begotten Son, Lord God, Lamb of God, Son of the Father, You take away the sins of the world, have mercy on us; You take away the sins of the world, receive our prayer; You are seated at the right hand of the Father, have mercy on us. For You alone are the Holy One, You alone are the Lord, You alone are the Most High, Jesus Christ, with the Holy Spirit, in the glory of God the Father. Amen.

PSALM 59:17-18

But I shall sing of Your strength, extol Your mercy at dawn, for You are my fortress, my refuge in time of trouble. My strength, Your praise I will sing; You, God, are my fortress, my loving God. Amen.

THE LORD'S PRAYER

Our Father who art in heaven, hallowed be Thy name. Thy kingdom come, Thy will be done on earth as it is in heaven. Give us this day our daily bread, and forgive us our trespasses, as we forgive those who trespass against us, and lead us not into temptation, but deliver us from evil. Amen.

MORNING OFFERING

O Jesus, through the Immaculate Heart of Mary, I offer You my prayers, works, joys and sufferings of this day for all the intentions of Your Sacred Heart, in union with the Holy Sacrifice of the Mass throughout the world, in reparation for my sins, for the intentions of all my relatives and friends, and in particular for the intentions of the Holy Father. Amen.

"If you invoke the Blessed Virgin when you are tempted, she will come at once to your help, and Satan will leave you." St. John Vianney

HAIL MARY

Hail Mary, full of grace,
the Lord is with thee.
Blessed art thou among women,
and blessed is the fruit of thy womb, Jesus.
Holy Mary, Mother of God,
pray for us sinners,
now and at the hour of our death. Amen.

DAY OFFERING

Father in Heaven, I give You today, all that I
think and do and say. And I unite it with all that
was done, by Jesus Christ Your Son. Amen.

GLORY BE

Glory be to the Father, and to the Son and to
the Holy Spirit. As it was in the beginning, is
now, and ever shall be, world without end.
Amen.

PRAYER OF ST. THOMAS AQUINAS

Grant me, O Lord my God,
a mind to know you,
a heart to seek you,
wisdom to find you,
conduct pleasing to you,
faithful perseverance in waiting for you,
and a hope of finally embracing you. Amen.

ST. PATRICK PRAYER

May the Strength of God pilot us.
May the Power of God preserve us.
May the Wisdom of God instruct us.
May the Hand of God protect us.
May the Way of God direct us.
May the Shield of God defend us.
May the Host of God guard us,
Against the snares of the evil ones,
Against temptations of the world.

May Christ be with us!
May Christ be before us!
May Christ be in us.
Christ be over all!
May Thy Salvation, Lord,
Always be ours,
This day, O Lord, and evermore. Amen.

ST. MICHAEL MORNING PRAYER

God be praised for the freshness of the morning and the dawning of this new day. Blessed Michael, we call upon your special custody over us. Please shield us from all bodily and spiritual peril. Help us to be truly Christian in today's activities and leisure moments. Inspire us to do good, to shun evil, and to remember how precious we are to the Giver of this new day. Amen.

A DAILY PRAYER TO THE SAINTS

Dear beloved Saint(s) _____, you are my friend(s) in Heaven. You guide me, you help me, you are there for me in my earthly journey.

As I live my life today, help me in my daily activities and direct me spiritually, so I can know and understand God's plan for me. Give me the grace and strength to assist those in need. Help me to care for those who need care.

Seek the Lord's blessing for me, so that I may experience God's love and goodness as you did, despite all the challenges and obstacles in daily life.

Ask God to grant me the courage and determination to always do what is right for me, my family, and those closest to me. Please hear my petitions and intercede for my special intentions before Our Loving Lord. *(State your request)*. Amen.

ST. FAUSTINA'S PRAYER

"Help me, O Lord,
... that my eyes may be merciful, so that I will never be suspicious or judge by appearances, but always look for what is beautiful in my neighbors' souls and be of help to them;
... that my ears may be merciful, so that I will be attentive to my neighbors' needs, and not be indifferent to their pains and moanings;
... that my tongue may be merciful, so that I will never speak badly of others, but have a word of comfort and forgiveness for all;
... that my hands may be merciful and full of good deeds;
... that my feet may be merciful, so that I will hasten to help my neighbor, despite my own fatigue and weariness;
... that my heart may be merciful, so that I myself will share in all the sufferings of my neighbor". Amen.

THE MEMORARE

Remember, O most gracious Virgin Mary, that never was it known that anyone who fled to your protection, implored your help, and sought your intercession, was left unaided. Inspired with this confidence, I fly unto you, O Virgin of virgins, my Mother, to you do I come; before you I stand sinful and sorrowful. O Mother of the Word Incarnate, despise not my petitions, but in your mercy hear and answer me. Amen.

PSALM 25:4-9

Make known to me Your ways, Lord; teach me Your paths. Guide me in Your truth and teach me, for You are God my savior. For You I wait all the long day, because of Your goodness, Lord. Remember Your compassion and love, O Lord; for they are ages old. Remember no more the sins of my youth; remember me only in light of Your love. Good and upright is the Lord, who shows sinners the way, guides the humble rightly, and teaches the humble the way. Amen.

A PRAYER FOR FIVE GRACES

My God, by the precious Blood of Jesus, grant me these five graces today: 1) The conversion of a sinner; 2) the conversion of a unbeliever; 3) the salvation of someone who is dying in danger of eternal damnation; 4) a vocation to the priesthood or to the religious life; 5) the grace for a new soul to have greater appreciation of the mystery of the Eucharist. Amen.

At the end of your prayer session make the **Sign of the Cross.**

THREE O'CLOCK PRAYERS

The Lord told St. Faustina: This is the hour of great mercy for the whole world. I will allow you to enter into My mortal sorrow. In this hour, I will refuse nothing to the soul that makes a request of Me in virtue of My Passion.

Make the **Sign of the Cross**.

MEDITITION

Meditate on the abandonment that Jesus felt during the agony in the garden.

THE PASSION PRAYER

Dear Lord Jesus,
by Your Passion and Resurrection
You brought life to the world.
But the glory of the Resurrection
came only after the sufferings of the Passion.
You laid down Your life willingly
and gave up everything for us.
Your body was broken and fastened to a Cross,

Your clothing became the prize of soldiers,
Your blood ebbed slowly but surely away,
and Your mother was entrusted to the beloved
disciple. Stretched out on the Cross, deprived of

all earthly possessions and human aid, You cried out to Your Father that the end had come. You had accomplished the work given You, and You committed into His hands, as a perfect gift, the little life that remained to You. Lord, teach me to accept all afflictions after the example You have given. Let me place my death in Yours and my weakness in Your abandonment, Take hold of me with Your love, that same foolish love that knew no limits, and let me offer myself to the Father with You so that I may rise with You to eternal life. Amen.

PASSION OF CHRIST, STRENGTHEN ME PRAYER

Passion of Christ, strengthen me! Strengthen me under the pressure of temptation. Strengthen me when principle is at stake. Strengthen me to do Your Will, My God. Strengthen me in moments of suffering, in times of loneliness, in periods of depression. Strengthen me that I may never swerve from You, dear Christ, nor weaken through human respect, through a desire to be popular, through hope of social distinction. Strengthen me to accept my cross and carry it generously to the end. On the battlefield of life, stand by me that I may never prove a traitor in the ranks. Stand by me that I may not be dazzled by the glitter and glow of the enemy camp. Amen.

PRAYER OF LOVE

God I love You,

Jesus I love You,
Blessed Mary ever virgin, please pray for me.

AWARENESS PRAYER

Lord, help me to better understand Your holy Passion. Help me to see the love that enabled You to endure such torment. May I see in Your Passion Your endless love for all and may I, in turn, love those who suffer with the same love I have for You. Jesus, I trust in You. Amen.

DIVINE MERCEY 3 O'CLOCK PRAYER

You expired, O Jesus, but the source
of life gushed forth for souls and an ocean of
mercy opened up for the whole world.
O Fount of Life, unfathomable Divine Mercy,
envelop the whole world and empty Yourself out
upon us.
O Blood and Water, which gushed forth from the
Heart of Jesus as a fount of mercy for us, I trust
in You. Amen.

Eternal Father, I offer Thee the Precious Blood
of Jesus, in satisfaction for my sins, and for the
needs of our Holy Church. Amen.

PRAYER BEFORE A CRUCIFIX

Look down upon me, good and gentle Jesus
while before Your face I humbly kneel and,
with burning soul,
pray and beseech You
to fix deep in my heart lively sentiments

of faith, hope, and charity;
true contrition for my sins,
and a firm purpose of amendment.
While I contemplate,
with great love and tender pity,
Your five most precious wounds,
pondering over them within me
and calling to mind the words which David,
Your prophet, said to You, my Jesus:
"They have pierced My hands and My feet,
they have numbered all My bones." Amen.

*If you have time, pray the Devine Mercy Chaplet
found on page 209.*

At the end of your prayer session make the **Sign
of the Cross.**

EVENING PRAYERS

Make the **Sign of the Cross.**

DOXOLOGY TO THE BLESSED TRINITY

Holy God, Holy Strong One,
Holy Immortal One, have mercy on us.
To You be praise,
to You be glory,
to You be thanksgiving
through endless ages,
O Blessed Trinity. Amen.

PSALM 9:2-3

I will praise You, Lord, with all my heart; I will declare all Your wondrous deeds. I will delight and rejoice in You; I will sing hymns to Your name, Most High. Amen.

THE LORD'S PRAYER

Our Father who art in heaven, hallowed be Thy name. Thy kingdom come, Thy will be done on earth as it is in heaven. Give us this day our daily bread, and forgive us our trespasses, as we forgive those who trespass against us, and lead us not into temptation, but deliver us from evil. Amen.

PRAYER OF ST. JEROME

O Lord, show Your mercy to me and gladden my heart. I am like the man on the way to Jericho who was overtaken by robbers, wounded and left for dead. O Good Samaritan, come to my aid. I am like the sheep that went astray. O Good Shepherd, seek me out and bring me home in accord with Your will. Let me dwell in Your house all the days of my life and praise You for ever and ever with those who are there. Amen.

PRAYER OF ST. JOHN OF VIANNEY

I love You, O my God, and my only desire is to love You until the last breath of my life. I love You, O my infinitely lovable God, and I would rather die loving You, than live without loving You. I love You, Lord and the only grace I ask is to love You eternally...My God, if my tongue cannot say in every moment that I love You, I want my heart to repeat it to You as often as I draw breath. Amen.

ST. AUGUSTINE PRAYER

You are great O Lord, and greatly to be praised: great is Your power, and of Your wisdom there is no end. In Your great mercy help me to cast out of my heart all sordid desires, greed, superstitions, blasphemies, and evil thoughts. Help me to throw away my resentments that I harbor against both my friends and my enemies. Make my heart worthy of Your love and help me lift my eyes to you in everything I do. Amen.

END OF DAY PRAYER

O my God, at the end of this day I thank You most heartily for all the graces I have received from You. I am sorry that I have not made a better use of them. I am sorry for all the sins I have committed against You. Forgive me, O my God, and graciously protect me this night. Blessed Virgin Mary, my dear heavenly mother, take me under your protection. St. Joseph, my dear Guardian Angel, and all you saints of God, pray for me. Sweet Jesus, have pity on all poor sinners, and save them from hell. Have mercy on the suffering souls in purgatory. Amen.

Briefly recall the good things that happened during the day with gratitude. Now make an examination of conscience. When finished, repent in sincere sorrow for the sins that you have reflected upon, then say an Act of Contrition.

ACT OF CONTRITION

O my God, I am heartily sorry for having offended Thee, and I detest all my sins, because I dread the loss of Heaven and pains of hell. But most of all because they offend Thee, my God, who are all good and deserving of all my love. I firmly resolve, with the help of Your grace, to sin no more and to avoid the near occasions of sin. Amen.

PROTECTION PRAYER

St. Michael, the Archangel, defend us in battle. Be our protection against the wickedness and snares of the devil. May God rebuke him, we humbly pray; and do you, O Prince of the heavenly host, by the power of God cast into hell Satan and all the evil spirits who prowl about the world seeking the ruin of souls. Amen.

Hail Mary... *(Say three times for an increase in the virtues of Faith, Hope and Charity.)*

PRAYER FOR THE POOR SOULS

Remember, O Lord, Thy servants and handmaids, N. and N., who have gone before us marked with the sign of faith and rest in the sleep of peace. To these, O Lord, and to all who rest in Christ, grant, we beseech Thee, a place of comfort, light, and peace. We ask this through Christ our Lord. Amen.

ST. PADRE PIO

O God, You gave Saint Pio of Pietrelcina, Capuchin priest, the great privilege of participating in a unique way in the Passion of your Son. Grant me through his intercession the grace of ... (Here mention your petition) which I ardently desire; And above all, grant me the grace of living in conformity with the death of Jesus, to arrive at the glory of the resurrection.

Glory be to the Father ... *(Say three times.)*

ANIMA CHRISTA
St. Ignatius of Loyola

Soul of Christ, sanctify me.
Body of Christ, save me.
Blood of Christ, inebriate me.
Water from Christ's side, wash me.
Passion of Christ, strengthen me.
O good Jesus, hear me.
Within Thy wounds hide me.
Never let me be separated from Thee.
From the malicious enemy defend me.
In the hour of my death call me, and bid me come unto Thee.
That with Thy saints I may praise Thee
Forever and ever. Amen.

ENLIGHTEN THE DARKNESS OF MY HEART
St. Francis of Assisi

O Most High, Glorious God, enlighten the darkness of my heart and give me a right faith, a certain hope, and a perfect love, understanding and knowledge, O Lord, that I may carry out Your holy and true command. Amen.

ST. AUGUSTINE'S NIGHT PRAYER

Watch, O Lord, with those who wake, or watch, or weep tonight, and give Your angels and saints charge over those who sleep. Tend Your sick ones, O Lord Jesus Christ. Rest Your weary ones. Bless Your dying ones. Soothe Your suffering ones. Pity Your afflicted ones. Shield Your joyous ones, and all for Your love's sake. Amen.

PRAYER FOR GENEROSITY

Lord, teach me to be generous,
to serve You as You deserve,
to give and not to count the cost,
to fight and not to heed the wounds,
to toil and not to seek for rest,
to labor and not to look for any reward,
save that of knowing that I do Your holy will.
Amen.

PRAYER FOR THE FORGOTTEN DEAD

O merciful God, take pity on those souls who have no particular friends and intercessors to recommend them to Thee, who, either through the negligence of those who are alive, or through length of time are forgotten by their friends and by all. Spare them, O Lord, and remember Thine own mercy, when others forget to appeal to it. Let not the souls which Thou hast created be parted from Thee, their Creator.

May the souls of all the faithful departed, through the mercy of God, rest in peace. Amen.

DEDICATION PRAYER

O my God, I thank You for having preserved me today and for having given me so many blessings and graces. I renew my dedication to You and ask Your pardon for all my sins. Amen.

PRAYER BEFORE SLEEP

O Great glorious God, grant me a safe restful sleep that I will awaken refreshed and eager to serve You. Amen.

At the completion of your prayer session make the **Sign of the Cross**.

PRAYERS FOR THE INTERCESSION OF SAINTS

ST. DYMPHNA

Lord, our God, you graciously chose St. Dymphna as patroness of those afflicted with emotional and nervous disorders. She is thus an inspiration and a symbol of charity to the thousands who ask her intercession. Please grant, Lord, through the prayers of this pure youthful martyr, relief and consolation to all suffering such trials, and especially those for whom we pray. *(Here mention them.)* We beg you, Lord, to hear the prayers of St. Dymphna on our behalf. Grant all those for whom we pray patience in their sufferings and resignation to Your divine will. Please fill them with hope, and grant them the relief and cure they so much desire. We ask this through Christ our Lord who suffered agony in the garden. Amen.

UNFAILING PRAYER TO ST. ANTHONY

O holy St. Anthony, gentlest of Saints, your love for God and charity for His creatures, made you worthy, when on earth, to possess miraculous powers. Encouraged by this thought, I implore you to obtain for me my request. *(Mention your petition.)* O gentle and loving St. Anthony, whose heart was ever full of human sympathy, whisper my petition into the ears of the Sweet Infant Jesus, who loved to be folded in your arms; and the gratitude of my heart will ever be yours. Amen.

ST. JUDE

O holy St Jude!
Apostle and Martyr,
great in virtue and rich in miracles,
near kinsman of Jesus Christ,
faithful intercessor for all who invoke you,
special patron in time of need;
to you I have recourse from the depth of my
heart, and humbly beg you, to whom God has
given such great power, to come to my assistance; help me now in my urgent need and grant
my earnest petition. *(Mention them.)* I will never
forget thy graces and favors you obtain for me
and I will do my utmost to spread devotion to
you. Amen.

St. PEREGRINE PATRON ST. OF CANCER

St. Peregrine, whom Holy Mother Church has
declared patron of those suffering from cancer, I
confidently turn to you for help in my present
sickness. I beg your kind intercession. Ask God
to relieve me of this sickness, if it be His Holy
Will. Plead with the Blessed Virgin Mary, the
Mother of Sorrows, whom you loved so tenderly
and in union with whom you have suffered the
pains of cancer, that she may help me with her
powerful prayers and loving consolation. But if it
should be God's Holy Will that I bear this sickness, obtain for me courage and strength to accept these trials from the loving hand of God
with patience and resignation, because He
knows what is best for my soul. Amen.

DIVINE MERCY CHAPLET
St. Faustina

Make the **Sign of the Cross**.
Our Father..., Hail Mary..., The Apostles Creed.

On the large bead before each decade say:
Eternal Father, I offer You the Body and Blood, Soul and Divinity of Your dearly beloved Son, Our Lord, Jesus Christ, in atonement for our sins and those of the whole world.

On the ten small beads of each decade:
For the sake of His sorrowful Passion, have mercy on us and on the whole world.

After the last decade, say the following prayer three times:
Holy God, Holy Mighty One, Holy Immortal One, have mercy on us and on the whole world.

NOVENA TO THE SACRED HEART OF JESUS

O my Jesus, You have said: "Truly I say to you, ask and you will receive, seek and you will find, knock and it will be opened to you." Behold I knock, I seek and ask for the grace of _____ *(name your request here)*.

Our Father . . . Hail Mary . . . Glory Be . . .
Sacred Heart of Jesus, I place all my trust in You.

IN SEARCH OF TRUTH

O my Jesus, You have said: "Truly I say to you, if you ask anything of the Father in my name, he will give it to you." Behold, in Your name, I ask the Father for the grace of _____ (name your request here).

Our Father . . . Hail Mary . . . Glory Be ...
Sacred Heart of Jesus, I place all my trust in You. Amen.

O my Jesus, You have said: "Truly I say to you, heaven and earth will pass away but my words will not pass away." Encouraged by Your infallible words I now ask for the grace of_____ (name your request here).

Our Father . . . Hail Mary . . . Glory Be . . .
Sacred Heart of Jesus, I place all my trust in You.

O Sacred Heart of Jesus, for whom it is impossible not to have compassion on the afflicted, have pity on us miserable sinners and grant us the grace which we ask of You, through the Sorrowful and Immaculate Heart of Mary, Your tender mother and ours.

Pray the **"Hail, Holy Queen"** (See page 124).

St. Joseph, foster father of Jesus, pray for us. Amen. *St. Margaret Mary Alacoque*

PADRE PIO'S PRAYER AFTER COMMUNION

Stay with me, Lord, for it is necessary to have You present so that I do not forget You. You know how easily I abandon You.

Stay with me, Lord, because I am weak and I need Your strength, that I may not fall so often.

Stay with me, Lord, for You are my life and without You I am without meaning and hope.
Stay with me, Lord, for You are my light and without You I am in darkness.

Stay with me, Lord, to show me Your Will.

Stay with me, Lord, so that I hear Your Voice and follow You.

Stay with me, Lord, for I desire to love You very much and always be in Your company.

Stay with me, Lord, if You wish me to be faithful to You.

Stay with me, Lord, as poor as my soul is I want it to be a place of consolation for You, a Nest of Love.

Stay with me, Jesus, for it is getting late and the day is coming to a close and life passes, death, judgment and eternity approaches. It is necessary to renew my strength, so that I will not stop along the way and for that, I need You. It is getting late and death approaches, I fear the darkness, the temptations, the dryness, the cross, the sorrows. O how I need You, my Jesus, in this night of exile!

Stay with me tonight, Jesus, in life with all its dangers, I need You. Let me recognize You as Your disciples did at the breaking of the bread, so that the Eucharistic Communion be the light which disperses the darkness, the power which sustains me, the unique joy of my heart.

Stay with me, Lord, because at the hour of my death, I want to remain united to You, if not by Communion, at least by grace and love.

Stay with me, Lord, for it is You alone I look for, Your Love, Your Grace, Your Will, Your Heart, Your Spirit, because I love You and ask no other reward but to love You more and more. With a firm love, I will love You with all my heart while on earth and continue to love You perfectly during all eternity. Amen.

ST. PIO'S THOUGHTS ON PRAYERS

"Prayer is the best weapon we have; it is the key that opens God's heart."

"Pray, hope and don't worry. Worry is useless. God is merciful and will hear your prayer."

ST. AUGUSTINE OF HIPPO

"Trust the past to God's mercy, the present to God's love, and the future to God's providence."

GLOSSARY

Abraham: The patriarch of Israel with whom God made a covenant. His given name was Abram. When Abram was ninety-nine years old, God made a covenant with him, changing his name to Abraham and promising to make him the "father of a host of nations"(Gen 17:1-8).

Absolution: A formal declaration given by a priest during the sacrament of Reconciliation (Penance) that a penitent's sins are forgiven.

Adultery: Sexual intercourse between a married person and another who is neither the husband nor wife. Adultery is a grievous sin forbidden by the sixth commandment.

All Saints' Day: A feast day celebrated on November 1 in honor of all the saints. It is a holy day of obligation.

Almsgiving: The giving of money or goods to the poor as an act of penance or Christian charity. The Church considers almsgiving one of the principal forms of penance.

Altar: A table on which the Sacrifice of the Mass is offered and is the focal point of the Church.

Amen: A solemn, prayerful affirmation signifying agreement with what has been said.

Angels: God's messengers to mankind. There are nine orders of angels: Angels, Archangels, Virtues, Powers, Principalities, Dominations, Throne, Cherubim, and Seraphim.[1]

Annunciation: When the angel Gabriel visited a virgin named Mary to inform her that she was to be the mother of our Savior Jesus as recorded in Luke 1:26-38.

Anointing of the Sick: One of the seven sacraments administered by a priest to Christians who are deathly sick to give spiritual aid and

---

[1] St. Gregory the Great, Hom. 34, in Evang.

perfect spiritual health. It is also known as extreme unction. This sacrament forgives sins, and also, conditionally, helps to restore the person's physical health.

Ascension: Forty days after Jesus' resurrection, the apostles witnessed the taking up of Jesus' glorified body into Heaven.

Ash Wednesday: The first day of Lent. It is a day of fast and abstaining from meat and is called Ash Wednesday because Catholics have their foreheads crossed with blessed ashes.

Assumption: The raising up of the Blessed Mother into Heaven. The Feast of the Assumption is celebrated on August 15.

Baptism, Sacrament of: The first of the seven sacraments in which, by water and the Word of God, a person is cleansed of all sin and reborn and sanctified in Christ to everlasting life.

Beatitudes: The promises of happiness preached by Christ in the Sermon on the Mount, for those who faithfully accept his teachings. The Beatitudes are recorded by St. Matthew (5:3-11) and by St. Luke (6:20-22).

Benediction: A Eucharistic devotion in which the consecrated Host is placed in a monstrance. The priest incenses it and a hymn is usually sung followed by a period of meditation, praise, and adoration by all.

Bible: The collection of books accepted by Christians as the authentic, inspired written record of the revelations made to man by God. The Bible is divided into two sections: the Old Testament, which contains forty-six books pertaining to the Old Covenant made with Abraham (in the Hebrew tradition) and the New Testament which contains twenty-seven books covering the New Covenant made with King David and the fulfillment of the coming of the Messiah, Jesus Christ. Etymology: Middle English, from Old French, from Medieval Latin *biblia*, from Greek, plural of *biblion* book, diminutive of *byblos papyrus*, book, from Byblos, ancient Phoenician city from which papyrus was exported.

Bishop: Derived from the Greek word *episkopos* meaning "overseer." A bishop is a successor of the apostles who has received the fullness of Christ's priesthood. He is normally in charge of a diocese and has the power to ordain priests.

Blasphemy: Speaking against God, the Church, or persons or things dedicated to God in a contemptuous, scornful, or abusive manner. These offenses may be committed by thought, word, or action. Blasphemy is a grave violation of charity toward God and violates the second commandment.

Blessed Sacrament: A name given to the Eucharist, one of the seven sacraments instituted by Christ to be received by the faithful.

Blessing: A blessing is a ceremony by which a deacon, priest, or bishop asks God to invoke divine favor on what he blesses. It usually consists of a short prayer, accompanied by the sign of the cross.

Calumny: Injuring another person's good name or reputation by lying. This is a very serious sin because it involves two sins in one: lying and injustice. To be truly sorry for this sin, one must work at restoring the injustice caused by one's lie.

Capital Sins: Sins towards which man in his fallen nature is inclined. There are seven: pride, avarice, envy, anger, gluttony, lust, and sloth.

Cardinal Virtues: There are four Cardinal virtues: prudence, justice, fortitude, and temperance. Each of these virtues has three parts defined as subjective, potential, and integral.

Catechism: The authoritative doctrinal manual of Catholic teachings.

Catechumen: A term used to describe one who is preparing for Baptism.

Catholic: Derived from the Greek word *katholikos*, meaning "universal."

Chalice: The cup used to hold the wine during Mass.

Charity: The theological virtue by which a person loves God above all things for his own sake and loves others for God's sake.

Chastity: One of the fruits of the Holy Spirit. Chastity is the moral virtue that moderates, according to the principles of one's faith and reason, the desire for sexual pleasure. In single people who wish to eventually marry, the desire is moderated by abstention until marriage; in those who decide never to marry, the desire must be sacrificed entirely.

Christ: The word "Christ," or *Christos* in Greek, is the equivalent of the Hebrew word *Messias,* which means "anointed." At the time of Jesus, it was used as a title rather than a name. Only after Jesus' Resurrection did the title gradually pass into a proper name, and the expression Jesus Christ or Christ Jesus become one designation.[2]

Christian: One who is baptized and professes to follow the teachings of Christ. In the New Testament, Acts 11:26 says, "it was in Antioch that the disciples were first called Christians."

Christ the King: A feast day, celebrated on the last Sunday of the Church's liturgical year, acclaiming Christ as King of the Universe. Pope Pius XI established the feast day in 1925.

---

[2] New Advent, "Origin of the Name of Jesus Christ," *Catholic Encyclopedia*, http://www.newadvent.org/cathen/08374x.htm.

Clergy: Those who have been ordained for divine service in the Church as deacons, priests, or bishops.

Communion of Saints: The spiritual unity that binds together the members of the Church on earth with the saints in Heaven and the souls in Purgatory as one Mystical Body with Christ at its head.

Confession: The voluntary confessing of one's sins to God through a qualified priest in order to obtain absolution from him.

Confessor: A priest who is qualified to hear confessions and grant sacramental absolution.

Confirmation: The sacrament, usually performed by a bishop, through which the laying on of hands, anointing with chrism, and prayer, one who is already baptized is strengthened by outpouring of the gifts of the Holy Spirit in order that one may confirm and steadfastly profess and live one's faith.

Conscience: The interior voice of the human intellect deciding, with faith and reason, the goodness or badness of an act. An educated and informed conscience moves one to choose to do what is right over doing evil.

Contemplation: A form of mystical prayer in which God supernaturally communicates to one's soul and intellect. This type of prayer is passive in nature, meaning it cannot be brought on by one's own effort but only as a gift given by God.

Contrition: The Council of Trent describes it as "a sorrow of soul and a hatred of sin committed, with a firm purpose of not sinning in the future." (Sess. XIV, ch. iv de Contritione).

Crucifix: A cross bearing the figure of the suffering or dead Jesus. It helps bring to mind the Passion of the Lord.

Days of Abstinence: The days prescribed by the Church on which one over the age of fourteen is forbidden to eat meat or any of its by-products. Ash Wednesday and all the Fridays in Lent, including Good Friday, are days of abstinence. All Fridays throughout the year, except holy days of obligation, are days of abstinence also, but one has the option to substitute another form of penance in its place.

Deacon: A level of the Holy Orders where a man is ordained to the ministry and service of the Church. The deacon's job is to assist the priest in preaching, baptizing, marrying others, and administrating in the parish.

Despair: The sin by which a person believes that one cannot cooperate with God's grace and gives up all hope for salvation.

Devil: A fallen angel. Commonly thought of as the leader of the fallen angels called Lucifer or Satan.

Diocese: A community of local Churches and the faithful, in communion of faith and sacraments with a bishop who has been ordained in apostolic succession.

Easter: The biggest feast day of the ecclesiastical year, and the day Christians celebrate Jesus' resurrection from the dead.

Encyclical: A document written by the Pope and sent to the bishops concerning matters related to the general welfare of the Church.

Envy: Resentment or sadness at another's success or good fortune. Envy is one of the seven capital sins.

Epiphany: The Feast of Epiphany celebrates the miracle of the star leading the magi from the East to adore Jesus, together with John the Baptist's baptizing Jesus in the Jordan, and the miracle that Jesus performed when He changed the water to wine at the wedding feast of Cana in Galilee.

Epistle: From the Greek word *epistole*, meaning "message" or "letter." In Mass the First Reading and Second Reading are called the Epistles.

Eucharist: To give thanks. It is one of the seven sacraments of the Church in which Jesus Christ during the consecration becomes present in the bread and wine for the reception of communion and for Jesus to be offered in the Sacrifice of the Mass, which is the center of the Church's life.

Eucharistic Prayer: The central part of the Mass, also known as the Canon, which contains the prayer of thanksgiving and the consecration.

Exorcism: Exorcism is (1) the act of driving out, or warding off, demons, or evil spirits, from persons, places, or things, which are believed to be possessed or infested by them, or are liable to become victims or instruments of their malice; (2) the means employed for this purpose, especially the solemn and authoritative adjuration of the demon, in the name of God, or any of the higher power in which he is subject.[3]

Fathers of the Church: Saintly teachers and writers of the early centuries who the Church recognizes as special witnesses to the faith and tradition of the Church.

Fornication: Sexual intercourse between an unmarried man and an unmarried woman. Fornication is a grievous sin.

Fortitude: Firmness of spirit, strength, or courage. It is one of the four cardinal virtues.

Gluttony: Over-indulging in food or drink. Gluttony is one of the seven capital sins.

Good Friday: The Friday before Easter on which the crucifixion of Jesus is commemorated. It is a day of fast and abstinence.

---

[3] Ibid., "Exorcism,"
http://www.newadvent.org/cathen/05709a.htm.

Gospels: The accounts of the birth, life, death, and resurrection of Jesus Christ as told in the oral tradition and later written down by the four evangelists: Matthew, Mark, Luke, and John. The Church believes and teaches that these four Gospels, when written, were inspired by God.

Grace: A supernatural gift given by God because of His disposition to do good to mankind to help with their eternal salvation, or a short prayer before meals thanking God for the food that one is about to eat. See chapter 15.

Hail Mary: A prayer known in Latin as the *Ave Maria* in which one asks the Blessed Mother to intercede. The first part contains the salutation of the angel Gabriel to Mary, and Elizabeth's greeting to Mary at the visitation, and the second part petitions her to pray for us.

Heaven: The dwelling place of God and the Blessed who have earned and received eternal life.

Hell: The state and or place of eternal punishment for those who through their own free will deliberately estranged themselves from the love of God. This includes the fallen angels.

Heresy: The denial or doubt after Baptism of an authorized teaching taught as truth by the Catholic Church.

Holy Days of Obligation: Feast days of the Church in which Catholics are obliged by

Church law to attend Mass and refrain from hard work.

Holy Saturday: Commemorates the day between Good Friday and Easter Sunday during which Jesus stayed within the tomb.

Holy Spirit (Holy Ghost): Also referred to as the Paraclete, Advocate, and the Spirit of Truth, the Holy Spirit is the third person of the Blessed Trinity. The Holy Spirit is distinct from the Father and the Son but is one in being and proceeds from the Father and from the Son.

Holy Thursday: Also called the Feast of Maundy, it is the Thursday of Holy Week when Catholics commemorate the Last Supper when Jesus established the Eucharist, the Sacrifice of the Mass, and the sacrament of the priesthood.

Holy Week: The week of Easter, beginning with Passion Sunday (Palm Sunday) and ending with Holy Saturday. It is the Church's annual celebration of Jesus' Passion, death, and resurrection.

Hope: The theological virtue by which we confidently expect, with God's help, to achieve both eternal life and the grace we need to attain it. Hope is an infused virtue, which cannot be obtained from one's own doing, but is given by God, as is the supernatural gifts of faith and charity.

Humility: The virtue by which a Christian maintains a modest estimate of his or her own worth, and his or her position with respect to God and others, while acknowledging that all good things come from God.

Incarnation: The incarnation is the dogma of the Word made Flesh: God becoming man. It is the union of the divine nature of the Son of God with the human nature of Jesus Christ as a person.

Immaculate: Without stain or blemish; spotless; undefiled.

Jesus: The Word made man. He was born of the Virgin Mary. He was crucified, suffered and died, and then rose from the dead and ascended into Heaven. Below are some symbols for the name "Jesus."

IHS: A Greek monogram of the name Jesus Christ.

INRI: The letters form the Latin inscription written on the cross stand for *Iesus Nazarenus Rex Iudaeorum*, or "Jesus of Nazareth, King of the Jews."

XP: A Greek monogram for *Christus*.

Joseph: Husband of the Blessed Mother Mary, venerated as a saint. The feast of Saint Joseph is celebrated on March 19.

Last Supper: The last meal taken by Christ and His disciples on the eve of His Passion at which He instituted the Holy Eucharist and the priesthood.

Lent: The liturgical season that begins with Ash Wednesday and ends with the celebration of the Paschal Mystery starting at sundown Holy Thursday. Lent is forty days in duration if you exclude Sundays and is a time of abstinence, fasting, and prayer.

Marriage: A permanent union of man and women by contract and vows. When both parties are baptized, it is called the sacrament of Matrimony.

Mary: The woman chosen by God to bring His Son into our world. Other names for Mary are Mother of God, Blessed Mother, Blessed Virgin Mary, the New Eve, and Mother of our Church.

Meditation: From the Latin word *meditatio*, meaning "thinking over." Meditation is a form of mental prayer, also known as discursive prayer, in which one uses his or her mind to think about God with emphasis on the role of the intellect reaching out and discovering God and His divine will.

Miracle: A work or wonder performed by supernatural power as a sign of some special mission or gift attributed to God.

Missal: A book containing prayers, songs, and text for the Mass.

Mortal Sin: A grievous sin, which separates one from God. It destroys sanctifying grace and causes the supernatural death of the soul. Also known as deadly, grave, and serious sin.

Moses: God's chosen one to lead the Israelites out of their exile in Egypt.

Mother of God: A title given to the Blessed Virgin Mary because she was chosen by God to bring his Son into the world.

Mystery: A truth that cannot be understood by human reason.

Natural Law: Laws from human nature that God has created in our world, to which everyone is subject and can grasp by human reason.

New Testament: The fulfillment of the Old Covenant in Jesus Christ. The New Testament is made up of twenty-seven different books attributed to eight different authors. Six of these authors were Jesus' apostles: Matthew, John, Paul, James, Peter, and Jude. The other two, Mark and Luke, were His immediate disciples.

Novena: from the Latin word *novem* meaning nine. It is a devotional prayer or series of prayers repeated for nine days.

Old Testament: The history of salvation starting with the world's creation up to the coming of Christ. The first forty-six books of the Bible, which the Catholic Church believes are divinely inspired. Also known as the Old Covenant with Israel

Original Sin: Also known as the sin of Adam, it was the direct disobedience of God by Adam. As a consequence of this sin, all humans lost holiness and became subject to the law of death. These effects were passed down through all his children, thus affecting the whole human race with the exception of Jesus and the Blessed Mother.

Palm Sunday: The Sunday before Easter. It is the last Sunday of Lent and starts the beginning of Holy Week. It commemorates Jesus' entering Jerusalem riding on the back of a donkey as His followers lined the streets waving palm branches in His honor. This Sunday is also known as Passion Sunday.

Parish: Normally located in a diocese, it is a territorial division that has been assigned its own priest by the bishop. The parish has its own church building and group of the faithful who live within the parish boundaries.

Penance: The conversion of one's heart by which one repents of his or her sins and is converted to living a life of God. Penance is also the punishment by which one atones for sins. These sins may be one's own or others'. These acts of penance normally include fasting, prayer, and almsgiving.

Penance (Reconciliation), Sacrament of: One's Sins committed after Baptism are confessed to God through a priest and then absolved by a priest in the name of God. Through the sacrament of Penance one's relationship with God is restored.

Pentateuch: The first five books of the Bible: Genesis, Exodus, Leviticus, Numbers, and Deuteronomy, thought to be written by Moses, also called the Torah.

Perjury: From the Latin word *periurium*, meaning "false oath" or "broken oath." Perjury is a serious sin because it disrespects God by calling on His name to witness as true what the perjurer knows to be false.

Prayer: The elevation of one's mind to God.

Pride: Pride is the excessive love of one's own accomplishments and worth and is one of the seven capital sins.

Priest: A man who is specially ordained as a minister "priest" to consecrate and offer the body and blood of Christ in the Mass and to administer the other sacraments.

Protestant: A person who has received a Christian baptism and believes in Christ, but does not profess the Catholic faith.

Prudence: A virtue by which one develops the knowledge to discern what is right from what is wrong. Prudence is acquired by one's own acts and given as a gift by God at the same time as sanctifying grace. It resides in the practical intellect.

Psalm: A sacred hymn of praise taken from the book of Psalms in the Old Testament.

Punishment, Temporal: The punishment that one receives either on earth or in Purgatory for sins committed, even though they have been forgiven in the sacrament of Reconciliation.

Purgatory: Comes from the Latin word *purgatio*, meaning "cleansing" or "purifying." Purgatory is a state in which the souls of the just are purified after death by the atoning for the temporal punishments due to their venial sins. It is the final cleansing of all human imperfections before entering Heaven.

Real Presence: Christ's presence in the Eucharist.

Reconciliation, Sacrament of: See Penance, Sacrament of.

Redeemer: A title for Jesus Christ, who through his death and resurrection redeemed all mankind.

Relativism: A view that ethical truths depend on the individuals and groups holding them.

Reparation: The act of making amends for a morally bad action. From the Latin word *reparare*, which means to "restore" or "to prepare anew."

Resurrection of Christ: The bodily rising of Jesus from the dead on the third day after His crucifixion and death on the cross and burial.

Sacrament: Sacrament is an outward sign of inward grace, instituted by Christ for the sanctification of souls. There are seven sacraments: Baptism, Reconciliation (Penance), the Eucharist, Confirmation, Holy Orders, Matrimony, and the Anointing of the Sick.

Sacred Heart: A symbolic representation of the physical heart of Jesus as the principal sign of His love for us and His Father.

Sacred Scripture: The sacred writings of the Old and New Testament that are believed to be inspired by the Holy Spirit.

Saint: One whom the Church honors as having lived a most virtuous life and who has gone to Heaven.

Salvation: Liberation from sin and its consequences.

Sanctifying Grace: A supernatural gift from God that makes holy those who receive it by giving them a participation in eternal salvation. Holiness and attaining eternal salvation depends solely upon the possession of sanctifying grace.

Satan: Leader of the fallen angels. Satan is the enemy of God and His people. Other names for Satan are the devil, Lucifer, Beelzebul, and Belial.

Savior: A title for Jesus Christ because He sacrificed His life for the salvation of mankind.

Seal of Confession: The requirement for the confessor to keep absolutely secret what a penitent has told to him in the sacrament of Penance.

Sermon: A talk given by the priest or deacon during Mass giving instruction in the Word of God. Also called a homily.

Sign of the Cross: A short prayer in which one makes a sign of the cross by touching the forehead, the breast, and the left and right shoulders with the right hand while reciting, "In the name of the Father, and of the Son, and of the Holy Spirit. Amen."

Sin: St. Augustine describes sin as "A word, deed or desire in opposition to the eternal law."

Sin of Adam: See Original Sin.

Sloth: Sluggishness or laziness in living a virtuous life. Sloth is one of the capital sins.

Son of Man: The title used by Christ himself in the Gospels. It appears eighty-one times in the Gospels and once in the book of Acts.

Soul: The spiritual part of a human being, which is created by God for each person and is infused into the body at the time of human insemination. Each soul is individual and immortal.

Sunday: The first day of the week. It is called the Lord's Day to commemorate Christ's resurrection from the dead. It is the day that Christians gather to celebrate the Eucharist.

Temperance: The moral virtue that controls the desire for pleasure.

Tradition: The "handing on" or passing down of God's revealed word that was not written in the Bible. The Church teaches, "It was done by the apostles who handed on, by the spoken word of their preaching, by the example they gave, by the institutions they established, what they themselves had received – whether from the lips of Christ, from His way of life and His works, or whether they had learned it by the prompting of the Holy Spirit."[4]

Transfiguration: When Jesus in the presence of His apostles Peter, James, and John was glorified. They saw Moses and Elijah appear and speak to Jesus and heard the voice of God.

---

[4] *Constitution on Divine Revelation*, II, 7.

Transubstantiation: A term used to describe the complete changing of the substance of bread and wine into the substance of the body and blood of Christ during the consecration by a validly ordained priest at Mass, so that only the accidents (the appearance) of bread and wine remain.

Triduum: A liturgical celebration of three days duration. A good example is the Easter Triduum, which consists of Holy Thursday, Good Friday, and Holy Saturday.

Trinity: The Trinity is the term employed to signify the central doctrine of the Christian religion -- the truth that in the unity of the Godhead there are Three Persons, the Father, the Son, and the Holy Spirit, these Three Persons being truly distinct one from another. Thus, in the words of the Athanasian Creed, "the Father is God, the Son is God, and the Holy Spirit is God, and yet there are not three Gods but one God." In this Trinity of Persons, the Son is begotten of the Father by an eternal generation, and the Holy Spirit proceeds by an eternal procession from the Father and the Son. Yet, notwithstanding this difference as to origin, the Persons are co-eternal and co-equal: all alike are uncreated and omnipotent. This, the Church teaches, is the revelation regarding God's nature which Jesus Christ, the Son of God, came upon earth to deliver to the world: and which she proposes to man as the foundation of her whole dogmatic system. [5]

Venial Sin: A minor offense against God, which does not mortally destroy the soul's relationship with God or deprive the sinner of sanctifying grace.

Vice: A strong tendency or habit in committing a gravely sinful act acquired through frequent repetition of the act. A morally bad habit.

Virgin Birth: The Church teaches that Mary, the mother of Jesus, was a virgin before, during, and after Jesus' birth. That Jesus was conceived by the Holy Spirit and born of the Virgin Mary.

Virtue: An operative habit that is essentially good, as distinguished from vice, which is an operative habit essentially evil.[6]

Vow: A promise made to God. A vow binds one under the pain of sin.

---

[5] New Advent, "The Blessed Trinity," *Catholic Encyclopedia*, http://www.newadvent.org/cathen/15047a.htm.
[6] Ibid., "Virtue," http://www.newadvent.org/cathen/15472a.htm.

INDEX

237

Books written by Chuck Gross

RATTLER ONE-SEVEN
A Vietnam Helicopter Pilot's War Story
© 2004

FIRST LIGHT
A POWs Rescue Mission That Can Never
Be Acknowledged
© 2013

MY DAILY PRAYER BOOK
©2018